THE JOHN HARVARD LIBRARY

BERNARD BAILYN
Editor-in-Chief

THE JOHN HARVARD LIBRARY

BONIFACIUS

AN ESSAY upon the GOOD

BY

Cotton Mather

Edited with an Introduction by
DAVID LEVIN

THE BELKNAP PRESS OF
HARVARD UNIVERSITY PRESS
CAMBRIDGE, MASSACHUSETTS
1966

CONTENTS

c

BONIFACIUS.

AN ESSAY
Upon the GOOD, that is to be
Devised and Designed,
BY THOSE
Who Desire to Answer the Great END
of *Life*, and to DO GOOD
While they *Live*.

A BOOK Offered,

First, in General, unto all CHRISTIANS,
in a PERSONAL Capacity, or in
a RELATIVE.

Then more Particularly,
Unto MAGISTRATES, unto MINISTERS,
unto PHYSICIANS, unto LAWYERS,
unto SCHOLEMASTERS, unto Wealthy
GENTLEMEN, unto several Sorts of
OFFICERS, unto CHURCHES, and
unto all SOCIETIES of a Religious
Character and Intention. With Humble
PROPOSALS, of Unexceptionable
METHODS, to *Do Good* in the World.

Eph. VI. 18. *Knowing that whatsoever Good thing any
man does, the same shall he receive of the Lord.*

BOSTON in *N. England*: Printed by B. Green, for
Samuel Gerrish at his Shop in Corn Hill. 1710.

INTRODUCTION

Bonifacius—usually known by its running title, *Essays to Do Good*—has always had a better reputation than the author who published it anonymously in 1710. It is Cotton Mather's historical fate to be considered largely as a transitional figure whose prodigious but narrow mind stretched inadequately between the zealous founding of the Bible Commonwealth and the enlightened struggle for the Republic. His efforts to retain the old Puritan values along with the old Puritan power have tended to diminish him in contrast to the giants who had first established that power in Boston. His advanced ideas on medicine, botany, education, philanthropy, and family discipline look like minor departures from reactionary principles when they are set beside the beliefs of eighteenth-century secular thinkers.

The habit of viewing Mather in the shadow of his potent ancestors began with his parents, who named him for his maternal grandfather, John Cotton, and it continued to affect his life until, in his sixtieth year, he wrote the life of his distinguished father, Increase Mather. When Cotton Mather was an eleven-year-old freshman at Harvard in 1674, his father became embroiled with other members of the Board of Overseers in a public battle that nearly destroyed the College. When the boy became at fifteen the youngest Harvard graduate, the President reminded him publicly of his duty to emulate not only his father but Richard Mather and John Cotton, his two famous grandfathers. Cotton Mather eventually devoted his entire life as a pastor to the very congregation that his father served as teacher. For forty years he worked closely with his father in various political controversies and social crises, from the loss of the colony's original charter, the rebellion against Sir Edmund Andros, the acceptance of a new charter, and the witchcraft trials, through debates about church government and membership and control of Harvard and Yale early in the new century. As a prolific historian, moreover, he wrote the lives of the first governors, the first ministers, the first Harvard presidents—the monumental church-history of New England, *Magnalia Christi Americana*.

Thus Mather unhappily observed the dissolution of the old theocracy even while he cheerfully did his best to extend pious influence in the community through his retrospective writings and his schemes for social action. At the same time, he labored enthusiastically in behalf of the new science. He sent reports of American phenomena to the Royal Society in London, which elected him a Fellow. He collected and published in New England the discoveries of European scientists. He persuaded a medical doctor to try inoculation during a smallpox epidemic in Boston. By the time he died in 1728, it was clear that the millennium he had so confidently predicted thirty years earlier was not yet to be expected. New England would have to settle instead for the imperfect Enlightenment.

For three centuries both Cotton Mather and his works have been discussed almost exclusively in this context of change. The church-history, we say, looks backward to Mather's grandfathers; *The Christian Philosopher* and *Bonifacius* look forward to Benjamin Franklin. Indeed, it was Franklin himself who first stressed the value of *Essays to Do Good* as a transitional document. In his very first published work Franklin paid Mather the tribute of parody by adopting the pseudonym of Mrs. Silence Dogood (counting on his Bostonian readers to know that the author of *Essays to Do Good* was rarely silent). Half a century later[1] Franklin told Samuel Mather that *Bonifacius* had turned his own youthful thoughts to methods of doing good, and again in his autobiography he acknowledged *Bonifacius* along with the works of Daniel Defoe and John Bunyan as one of the most valuable influences on his early thought. The relationship would be evident even if Franklin had not written so explicitly. Commentators have repeatedly cited it ever since George Burder quoted Franklin's letter to Samuel Mather in an English edition of *Essays to Do Good* (London, 1807).

Insistence on such historical relationships has taught us much about the changes from pious Puritanism to moralism, from striving in the world for the glory of God to striving for enlightened self-interest. But this perspective has also done considerable harm. Students of historical change have often blurred our understanding of Franklin's and Mather's individual minds and books. The intense light focused on one set of eighteenth-century statements has left others in the darkness. Mather, especially, has been projected so rigidly against what he looked back to, or what he anticipated, that it is unusually difficult to discover what he was.

The modern reader of *Bonifacius* must be prepared to recognize two influential versions of this distortion. The first concerns Puritan piety; the second, Puritan commercial ethics and benevolence.

Perry Miller's magnificent volumes on *The New England Mind* argue that the earliest New England Puritans temporarily united pious faith and reasoned, vigorous action under a grand modification of Abraham's Covenant. The second volume dramatizes the inevitable separation of faith from thought and the inevitable subordination of faith as the Covenant dissolves under the pressure of seventeenth-century events in Europe and America. Cotton Mather is the pivotal figure in Miller's narrative of historical change. At first he preaches jeremiads, long sermons condemning the sins of the land. But as he and other clergymen lose political power in the early decades of the eighteenth century, Mather resorts to new devices, both social and psychological. Now he abandons the jeremiad. Renouncing hope of political power, he tries instead to influence events by publishing "pietist" instructions for communal life, including proposals for voluntary associations to reform morals. Privately, moreover, he takes emotional refuge from the religious decline of New England by retreating often to his study; there, according to Miller, Mather tries to "stimulate" his overwrought nervous system to a factitious piety that seeks explicit, divine assurances and demands prostrate, methodical prayer and fasting. In this analysis his correspondence with such foreign reformers as Auguste Francke of Halle is an accidental consequence of Mather's compulsive scribbling and of his response to New England's needs and his own. It has nothing to do with international pietist movements of the time. Mather, indeed, is astonished to find himself in the vanguard, an agent of the new pietism.

Miller presents *Bonifacius* as a milestone on the downward road from John Winthrop to Dickens' caricature of nineteenth-century utilitarianism, Thomas Gradgrind, and he contends that Cotton Mather was further from Winthrop than from Gradgrind. *Bonifacius*, he concedes, is "not quite a surrender of piety to business," but he declares that Mather found in *Bonifacius* "a new form of marketing religion." He describes Mather's appeal to the inherent reward of doing good as a sentimental invitation to luxuriate in the "delicious swooning joy of the thing itself." He sees Mather's voluntary associations not as part of an effort to liberate New Englanders but as an attempt to reassert clerical control, and he associates Mather with those service clubs (from the Y.M.C.A. to the Rotary) that work for conformity of various kinds in modern America.[2]

The chief trouble with this interpretation is that it is almost completely subservient to a generalization about the decline in piety. It cannot admit the possibility that Cotton Mather was as pious as his ancestors; it insists on explaining his piety as a neurotic, belated reaction to historical events that occurred when he was past thirty.

The consequent distortion of *Bonifacius* begins at the beginning, with Mather's title. Because of our modern interest in placing Mather on the line from Puritanism to utilitarianism, scholars have customarily shortened the original title of *Bonifacius* in a way that changes its significance. *Bonifacius*, they have called it; *an Essay upon the Good that is to be Devised and Designed by Those who Desire . . . to Do Good While they Live.* This seems in any case a strangely illogical title—as if there were others, *besides* those who desire to do good, who should devise and design good! The important distortion, however, is the change in Mather's purpose. He did not really write for those who desire to do good but for those who desire "to Answer the Great End of Life," and who *therefore* desire to do good while they live.

The great end of life, for Cotton Mather as for John Winthrop before him and Jonathan Edwards after, was not to do good but to glorify God. Mather had made this plain from the beginning of his career as a preacher, and at the height of his political power. Just after he had served as one of the chief conspirators to overthrow the tyrant Sir Edmund Andros in 1689, he published a volume of sermons at the request of his wealthy father-in-law, John Philips, who on recovering from a serious illness had offered to subsidize the publication of four sermons on "Practical Godliness." None of these sermons is a jeremiad. All relate devotional piety to doing good:

> The chief end of man is to *glorify* God . . . To praise God is to *render* and *procure* a due acknowledgment of His excellence . . . This, this *praise* of the LORD is the *end* of our *life* in the world.
> This is the *end* of our *being*. We are told that *we have our*

being *in God.* Of all things whatever this is then most reasonable, *that we should have our* being *for* God; and our being *for* Him, is not expressed without our praising of Him . . . Every man should say: "I *live* that God who is worthy to be *praised,* may have the *praises* of my obedience to Him."

The saints in Heaven, Mather says in the same sermon, have their appropriate way of praising God, by "shouting Hallelujah, Hallelujah, before the Throne"; but men living on earth have special, additional ways of praising Him here: "by the discharge of many *relations,* which the dead saints are strangers unto. We may *now* praise God as *parents,* as *masters,* as *officers* in the Church or Common-wealth. All those capacities shall *die* with us . . . "³

In these sermons there is no tension between doing good and praising God. Doing good is one way of praising Him. Of course, we can find sentences that support the emphasis on practical striving in the world: "To *serve God* was the very errand which we were brought into the wilderness upon"; "the service of God is His worship"; "there are two things incumbent upon us, to do good and to get good." But the good we are to get is the capacity to enjoy God. Lifting such statements out of their pious context is a serious error. Although it may indicate those subtle changes of emphasis that eventually prevailed in American life when the idea of God's sovereignty had been weakened, it can misrepresent not only individual books and the condition of individual minds, but at last the very history that such abstractions were meant to serve.

As early as 1689, then, Cotton Mather had set forth the principle on which he would organize *Bonifacius* twenty years later.⁴ He would begin with the reformation of the self and would then move outward into the community, suggesting methods of service in the various "relations" of life. In the intervening years he often followed this procedure in composing biographies. Thus his life of John Eliot opens outward from personal piety to family government to preaching in the church, and finally to Eliot's evangelism among the Indians.

The organization communicates the central purpose: to praise God in every act of life. By 1688 Mather had adopted the "delightful and surprising way of thinking" that he attributed to his deceased younger brother Nathanael. His language suggests that he was perhaps as close to Jonathan Edwards and to Emerson, Thoreau, and Whitman as he was to Thomas Gradgrind: Nathanael Mather, Cotton Mather wrote, "considered that the whole *Creation* was full of God; and that there was not a leaf of *grass* in the field, which might not make an observer to be sensible of the Lord. He apprehended that the *idle minutes* of our lives were many more than a short liver should allow: that the very filings of *gold*, and of time, were exceeding precious; and, that there were little *fragments of hours* intervening between our more stated businesses, wherein our *thoughts* of God might be no less pleasant than frequent with us." [5] Just as Henry Thoreau would later tell New England's time-passing knitters that it is impossible to kill time without injuring eternity, Mather warned busy Bostonians that God would "find an *eternity* to *damn* the man that cannot find a *time* to *pray*." [6]

The terms in which Mather implored Christians to "redeem time" show that his pietism was in full vigor in 1682, before he was twenty and before the original charter of Massachusetts Bay had been revoked. He was taking John Winthrop's original message to the community but with a new emphasis on method, on the deliberate saturation of one's life in pious action, and especially on ingenuity. "Thus be *zealous of good works, work for God*," he said in 1689. "Let even your *eating*, your *trading*, your *visiting*, be done as a *service* for the Lord, and let your *time*, your *strength*, your *estates*, all the *powers* of your spirits and all the *members* of your bodies be ingeniously laid out in that *service*. Often ask your own souls, *What is there that I*

may do for God? Even court, and hunt advantages to be serviceable . . ." [7]

The origins of Mather's interest in such hunting lie deep in
seventeenth-century Protestant pastoral work. To understand
his career we must remember that Cotton Mather was the *pastor*
in the Boston church which his father served as teacher, and that
he therefore had a special duty to attend to the people's daily
needs. From the beginning of his professional life, he had a remarkable opportunity to apply his great energy over the whole
range of Bostonian life. His social action began with secluded
meditations in which, with the occasional aid of specific assurances from an angel, he prayed for divine support of afflicted
parishioners and of Massachusetts battles against the Devil and
the French; it extended to the writing of histories and biographies, to joining the leadership of a revolution, to advising governors, addressing the legislature, offering medical advice, curing the bewitched child of a parishioner, making pastoral visits,
catechizing children, administering church discipline to offend-
ing members of the congregation, and writing books to teach
the most ordinary people methods of becoming Christians and
then practicing Christianity in their daily lives.

For some of this work a number of English writers had provided valuable guides. Cotton Mather and his brother Nathanael
were especially fond of Joseph Hall's *Occasional Meditations*
(3d edition, 1633), William Waller's *Divine Meditations* (1680),
Henry Scudder's *The Christian's Daily Walk* (1628). Cotton
Mather also borrowed from Richard Baxter's immense folio
Christian Directory (1673) and *How to Do Good to Many;
or, the Public Good is the Christian's Life* (1682).

All these books have in common with Mather's efforts a determination to bring the common into touch with the divine. Hall's
meditations, which both Nathanael and Cotton Mather emu-
lated, drew religious lessons from such conventional earthly experiences as "the sight of a grave digged up," "gnats in the sun,"

INTRODUCTION

"the sight of a drunken man," "bees fighting," "the sight of a
piece of money under water," "a defamation dispersed." Ready
to let every leaf of grass make him sensible of the Lord,
Nathanael Mather notes that a kettle of water taken from the
fire in a cold New England room is quickly "seized with luke-
warmness." So, he concludes, are Christians after they have been
warmed by some awareness of God's glory. When John Winthrop interprets the killing of a snake during a synod meeting
or Nathanael Mather jumps from his "bed of security," braving
the cold to put on "Christ's garments" and walk to the fire, the
lesson in this literary form is always made explicit, and the value
of the meditation depends on the aptness of explicit parallels.
This is a principle Benjamin Franklin kept in mind when he
perfected a quite different kind of anecdote a century later in
his autobiography.

In a book like *Bonifacius* the method is reversed. The pastor,
accustomed to studying minor events for evidence of God's
will, now uses his ingenuity to find explicit ways in which a
Christian can express the benevolence with which grace has endowed him. Christians need to be told *how* to do good, especially when they live outside the traditional authority of a
hierarchical church and in a swiftly changing society. Yet the
movement should not be seen simply as a weakening of old
Calvinist reliance on faith and predestination. It seems instead
a natural extension of the kind of impulse that led Puritans to
establish the New England colonies in the first place. Once the
community of saints has established its right to exist, it must
set about expanding God's work in the world. "Though God
set up lights so small as will serve but for one room, and though
we must begin at home, we must far more esteem and desire the
good of multitudes," Baxter said, and we must set "no bounds to
our endeavors, but what God and disability set." *Bonifacius*
echoes: the magistrate is "the *Minister of God for good*. His
empty name will produce a *cruel crime*, if he don't set himself

xv

to do good, as far as ever he can extend his influences." Americans in the second half of the twentieth century have seen this kind of rhetoric applied to vast proposals for a Great Society at home and for aid to multitudes in Asia.

For Cotton Mather, moreover, the millennium was not a metaphor for secular achievement. It was literally imminent. He wrote quite seriously, on the one hand, about exactly how the righteous in America might be spared from the fires sweeping the earth before the establishment of the Kingdom here.[8] And he did his best, in the year he wrote *Bonifacius,* to see that Bostonians accepted "the true doctrine of the Chiliad" so that, by eliminating all "base dealing"—all "dirty ways of dishonesty"—from the market place, they might make their street as golden as the one promised in the Book of Revelations from which he had taken his text. He preached this sermon to the General Assembly of the colony, before whom he "proclaimed unto all the world" that "ill-dealings are not at all countenanced; no, they are vehemently disallowed, by the religion of NEW-ENGLAND." The gold he referred to was not profit but precept; "The street of the city is pure gold" meant to him that "the business of the CITY, shall be managed by the *Golden* Rule. The things that use to be done in the market-place, shall be done without *corruption.*" [9]

It is in this context that we must consider the second historical distortion of Mather's ideas. Just as emphasis on the decline of piety may overlook his concentration on divine glory, so efforts to trace the Protestant Ethic can ignore not only the divine object of human striving but also his thorough conviction of community. A. Whitney Griswold, in an important essay published more than thirty years ago,[10] cited impressive evidence to show that Mather stressed the Christian's obligations to work diligently in his calling; Mather repeated the Biblical promise (so effective with Benjamin Franklin) that the young man who was diligent would stand before kings, and he urged the young man who wished to rise *by* his business to rise *to* his business. But although Griswold scrupulously links this personal calling with the general vocation of a Christian, his interest in linking Mather's advice to the "rugged individualism" of a later time ignores the perfectly explicit condemnation of all sharp dealing and dishonesty in financial affairs. Mather insisted that New England's professions of extraordinary religion would be worthless if its "dealing" should be "defective in honesty . . . Let a man be never such a professor and pretender of *religion,* if he be not a *fair-dealer,* THAT MAN'S RELIGION IS VAIN. A noise about *faith and repentance,* among them that forget MORAL HONESTY, 'tis but an empty noise. The men are utter strangers to *faith* and *repentance* . . . Woe, woe, woe, to you professors, and HYPOCRITES, who can make a show of this and that piety, and *purity;* but can *cheat,* and *cozen,* and *oppress,* and wrong other people in your dealing with them!" [11]

Far from supporting rugged individualism, Mather declared that the Golden Rule should have its application to business through the Scriptural command of Paul (I Corinthians 10:24): *"Let no man seek his own, but every man another's wealth."* Lying was to be forbidden, all dealings were to be "transparent glass," and neither the foolish nor the poor were to be exploited: "For men to *overreach* others, because they find them *ignorant,* or screw grievously upon them, only because they are poor and low, and in great necessities; to keep up the *necessaries* of human life (I say the necessaries, which I always distinguish from the *superfluities*) at an immoderate price, merely because other people want them, when we can easily spare them; *'tis an abomination!"* For necessities, at least, the law of supply and demand was not supreme.[12]

Thus, although Mather confessed that he knew neither the niceties nor the mysteries of the market place, he did not rest content with prescribing the Golden Rule. Stating that imperative even in its most positive form [13] would hardly forbid ruth-

less competition if the individual merchant should be willing to
have his neighbor compete just as fiercely as himself. Mather did
not supply an ethic fit for the mysteries and niceties, but he did
condemn many commercial "abominations," from the slave
trade ("one of the worst kinds of thievery in the world") to the
adulteration or misrepresentation of a large number of specified
products.[14]

It was a theological principle that gave Mather's sense of community its importance in practical affairs, in his day as well as
through the later teachings of Franklin. To consider the principle we must enter that dizzy world of circular argument and
begged questions in which Puritans struggled to distinguish
faith from works without becoming either antinomians or (to
use a word from *Bonifacius*) merit-mongers.

In that world a Christian must recognize a central paradox:
his assurance of salvation depends on his renouncing all claims to
salvation that place any confidence or value in himself. He must
become convinced that he does not deserve salvation and that
he cannot earn it. If convinced of his inadequacy but unable to
attain a conviction of faith, he may fall into the sin of despair,
a beginning of Hell on earth. If he does find a conviction of
Christ's power and willingness to redeem him, he must test the
conviction by regularly examining his attitude and his conduct.
Good works cannot save him—indeed, no works are truly good
unless they proceed from a justifying faith—but the consequence of true faith is a benevolence that impels the converted
sinner to praise God through obedient service. *Bonifacius* declares, therefore, that "a workless faith is a worthless faith."

Historians gain some value from turning this process around
(as some busy, conscientious sinners must have done) to mean
not only that worklessness proved worthlessness but also that
works proved worth. Often, however, the reversal costs too
much, for it blocks appreciation of the great power in one of
the chief articles of American faith. The great power comes

from the conviction that what is right, works. Both Mather and Franklin worked to propagate this conviction, and both appealed to the reader's self-interest, but neither man ever contended that whatever works is right. Mather and other Puritans actually believed that prosperity could be as threatening a Providential judgment as calamity. Merciful dispensations, Mather said, "are so many trials whether we will hear God speaking in our prosperity; or whether when we wax fat we will kick against the Lord."

For many people, at least, the drama of guilt, self-doubt, and self-accusation was a terrible reality, and so, too, was the kind of faith that Mather preached. (Even Franklin recognized it during the Great Awakening.) Once that reality stands at the center of our attention, we need not be religious to understand Mather's declaration that good works are a part of, as well as prescribed steps along the way to, "the great salvation." The penitent sinner who wanted to join the church might be crushed (in Edward Taylor's phrase) between desire and fear—between a longing to profess his conversion and fear that it is delusory. Having experienced this kind of paralysis, the conscientious sinner might well be grateful for rescue, even in this world, from the psychological self-torture of futility. The ability to act might well be the worldly consequence of such faith.

Not only the motive but the social consequence, too, is a principle or a power rather than a quantitative fact. Just as Mather and Franklin, despite their obvious differences, worked outward from the idea of virtue, gratitude, duty, and wisdom to acts of service, so they conceived of the good done to others as a beginning rather than as charity in the limited sense of alms. *Bonifacius* cites the primitive Church's doctrine that the sin of a Christian's neighbor is a sin by the Christian himself. As Richard Baxter ordered Christians to succor poor men's bodies in order to make it possible to save their souls,[15] Mather argues that the American Indians must be "civilized" so that they can be "Christianized." He praises the English philanthropist Thomas Gouge for finding work for the poor, and he commands his own readers to "find 'em work, set 'em to work, keep 'em to work." Benjamin Franklin says it is hard for an empty sack to stand upright.

In these years both Old and New England had need of the ingenuity to which Mather appealed. The vigorous new capitalist organizations in "this projecting age" gave such different authors as Richard Baxter, Daniel Defoe, Jonathan Swift, Cotton Mather, and (by the early 1720's) Benjamin Franklin examples of mutual cooperation that might be used for the public good. Baxter's *Christian Directory* directed Christians "How to Improve all Helps and Means" toward a Christian life in the world. Defoe's *Essay on Projects* (1697) proposed Friendly Societies for several kinds of life and medical insurance; Swift's ironic *A Project for the Advancement of Religion and the Reformation of Manners* (1709) suggested a scheme for institutionalizing virtue through the Queen's power of preferment and the Court's leadership of fashion.

In England the Societies for the Reformation of Manners had already come under suspicion as petty meddlers by the time Swift published this proposal, but the social need for such organizations seems more interesting than the modern temptation to think of their motives as simply repressive. Systematic welfare programs were of course unknown. Widespread drunkenness seems to have been a relatively new problem, and it existed in a context that may now be difficult to imagine. Wine was often poisonously adulterated; alcoholic and other debtors and petty criminals were locked up indiscriminately in prisons in which conditions were far more abominable than the worst kind of do-gooding. Epidemics in these foul places sometimes made the punishment for civil offenses as lethal as the capital penalty officially attached to so many crimes. There was no

effectively organized, properly trained, or trustworthy police
force to prevent the growing number of violent crimes on city
streets, which were generally unlighted. Private citizens armed
to defend themselves. Two years after *Bonifacius* was published,
a group of drunken young men who called themselves Mo-
hocks terrorized London with atrocious beatings and mutilations
that seemed the more terrible because they were apparently
unmotivated.

I do not mean to contend that life in Queen Anne's London
was a nightmare. The point is that specific needs in the society,
needs unmet by government or other established organizations,
encouraged the new techniques for organized benevolence and
that in the absence of better preventive methods religious
writers naturally encouraged Christians to set an individual example. Nor should we forget, even when considering the restric-
tive nature of some actions, the disastrous consequences of in-
discretions that may seem minor today. Under the prevailing
Canon Law, for example, it was easy to find oneself entrapped
in a virtually indissoluble marriage, and many Londoners—
sailors and young gentlemen alike—suffered from a lucrative
conspiracy of clergyman, landlord, prostitute, and lawyer. In
such circumstances advice against drinking, which neither
Cotton nor Increase Mather ever opposed in its moderate form,
and advice against falling into debt need not be officious. Med-
dlesomely repressive though they might become, societies like
Mather's Young Men's Associations, Count Zinzendorf's Slaves
of Virtue, and Benjamin Franklin's projected Society of the
Free and Easy grew out of a positive desire to free men for the
practice of virtue in this world.

What we need to remember, then, is the firmness with which
Mather's good-doing is tied to the praise of God, the certainty
with which his exhortations to be diligent rely on traditional
ethics. *Bonifacius* is addressed to Christians; Mather invites un-
believers to close the book until, by repentance, they begin to

live. He is not marketing religion but bringing religion into the market.

Besides a few specific ideas, which deserve separate attention, the key value of *Bonifacius* lies in the resourceful application of methodical ingenuity to pious affairs. Christians, Mather says, should employ their wits for God's service. As Thoreau will later complain that farmers speculate in herds of cattle in order to acquire shoestrings, Mather charges New Englanders with wasting grand capacities on trivial ends. He exhorts them to apply to good works the same ingenuity noted in their business affairs, to equal the degree of contrivance (without the deception) employed by the Devil and the wicked in pursuit of evil ends.

Bonifacius thus appeals simultaneously to one of the most powerful traits in the New England character and to one of the strongest intellectual forces of the eighteenth century. Mather invokes for his divine purpose the desire to invent new means, to contrive, devise, experiment. Nor does he content himself with precepts. He repeatedly sets the example, for the impulse has come from one of the most powerful sources of his own conduct.

Scholarship has rarely found a less appropriate figure than the cliché that says Cotton Mather's knowledge was undigested. Ever since the early 1680's Mather had been scribbling in private as well as for publication, and he worked hard to reduce his experience and his knowledge to usable form. In his *Quotidiana*, copybooks in which he recorded scraps of quotations, scientific curiosities, and historical ancedotes, he laboriously compiled indexes so that he would be able to call on the information in his sermons and other works. In his conversation, moreover, he was remarkably quick to apply his diverse knowledge with an ingenuity that was sometimes startling. His diary, Paterna,[16] and *Bonifacius* demonstrate that this quality was more than a natural aptitude. He hunted advantages for pious service in conversation, in idle moments of dinner parties, in the observance of various people as he walked the streets. And of course he wrote down the suggestions, which ranged from prayers to be said on seeing a beautiful woman, and resolutions to drop the name of a poor parishioner when visiting a rich one, to planning the conversation at his family's meals so that the children would be instructed.

It is easy to treat this carefully nurtured habit as comically tasteless by selecting one detail, such as Mather's resolution to meditate while urinating. Even when we supply the context for this example and notice that Mather feared the excruciating pain of kidney stones, which had tortured his grandfather, many of us will find it difficult to accept his resolution to offer up thanks, while urinating, for the grace that has spared him from his grandfather's affliction. Such a meditation can be defended, too, but the criticism misses the point. What matters is the total concentration on developing the discipline of pious resourcefulness. For every ludicrous example there is a passage that seems successful. Benjamin Franklin reports that when he accidentally hit his head on a beam in Mather's house, Mather told him to stoop always as he walked through life, so that he would save himself many a hard thump. Mather resolves in Paterna never to offer his children play as a reward for hard work, lest they come to consider diversion better than diligence. Instead he contrives to punish them by refusing to teach them something, and he resolves to reward them by teaching them "some curious thing."

Nor was there any hesitation to work out a much more elaborate meditation relating to recent scientific theories. A long paragraph from Paterna will illustrate the kind of personal resolution that led Mather to write his Christian Philosopher. Here he comes very close to using eighteenth-century science in precisely the way that ennobles the works of Jonathan Edwards:

I am continually entertained with *weighty body*, or *matter* tending to the *center of gravity:* or attracted by matter. I feel it in my own. The *cause* of this *tendency,* 'tis the glorious GOD! *Great GOD, Thou givest this matter such a tendency; Thou keepest it in its operation!* There is no other cause for *gravity*, but the *will* and *work* of the glorious GOD. I am now effectually convinced of that ancient confession, and must effectuously make it, "He is not far from every one of us." When I see a thing moving or settling that way which its *heavy nature* carries it, I may very justly think, and I would often form the thought, "It is the glorious GOD who now carries this matter such a way." When *matter* goes *downward*, my spirit shall therefore mount *upward*, in acknowledgment of the GOD who orders it. I will no longer complain, "Behold, I go forward, but He is not there; and backward, but I cannot perceive Him: on the left hand, where He does work, but I cannot behold Him: He hideth Himself on the right hand, that I cannot see Him." No, I am now taught where to meet with Him; even at every turn. *He knows the way that I take;* I cannot stir forward or backward, but I *perceive* Him in the *weight* of every *matter*. *My way* shall be to improve this as a *weighty argument* for the being of a GOD. I will argue from it, "Behold, there is a GOD, whom I ought forever to love and serve and glorify." Yea, and if I am tempted unto the doing of any wicked thing, I may reflect, that it cannot be done without some *action*, wherein *the power of matter* operates. But then I may carry on the reflection: "How near, how near am I to the glorious GOD, whose commands I am going to violate! Matter keeps His laws; but, O my soul, wilt thou break His laws? How shall I do this wickedness and therein deny the GOD, who not only is above, but also is exerting His power in the very matter upon which I make my criminal misapplications!" [17]

The very repetitiousness of Mather's inexhaustible pen demonstrates the persistence of his search for advantages to do good methodically, ingeniously. Besides recording his resolutions, drawing up proposals, preparing indexes, he completely

revised his annual diaries so that they might be useful to other
readers. Then he copied the relevant portions of these revised
versions into Paterna, for his son, and he copied relevant inci-
dents, some of them extensive, into *Bonifacius*, making appropriate revisions. At his death he left two grand unpublished
books, The Angel of Bethesda and *Biblia Americana*, which
form part of this same resolute plan. The Angel of Bethesda is
a collection of medical advice and cures incorporating the kind
of spiritual usefulness proposed in *Bonifacius*, and *Biblia
Americana* condenses, with Mather's own contributions, centuries of commentary on the Bible.

The energy that performed such prodigies undoubtedly drew
some strength from vanity as well as from piety. Although
Bonifacius was published anonymously, Mather's effort to seem
expert in varied professional subjects will seem amusingly pre-
tentious to modern readers, especially when he alludes to legal
authors. Yet the conscious purpose of such allusions is to win the
respect of those to whom the author offers moral advice useful
in their professions, and to exemplify the kind of ingenuity he
has been prescribing. The author of *Bonifacius* has taken the
trouble to inform himself of at least a few good books and a few
specific means for lawyers to do good. In medicine, Mather
had no less training and was better read than many practicing
physicians.

The pastor's concern with social health leads Mather to express in *Bonifacius* a number of ideas that would be interesting
to modern readers even outside the context I have tried to establish. He declares that none but a good man really lives, and that
one becomes more alive as one acts for good. Concern for the
soul and interest in method lead him to encourage rewards
rather than punishment in educating children. He opposes
beating except for the most serious offenses. He condemns
tyrannical schoolmasters as a curse. He advises ministers to
preach on subjects of particular use to their congregations and

to ask the people to suggest topics for sermons. He favors the practical education of girls. He advises physicians to treat the poor without charge and to attend not only to the patient's soul but also to the "anxiety" that may be causing his illness. He tells lawyers never to appear in a dirty cause, always to eschew sharp tricks, and to defend the principle of restitution. He condemns that usury which charges interest for money that the debtor never gets to use. He tells the rich to use their money for good while they live, rather than leave large estates.

All these proposals issue from the same pious concern that asks landlords to oblige their tenants to pray, pious societies to look out for their neighbors' sins, schoolmasters to teach Duport's verses on Job instead of Homer. What we must seek if we wish to know Mather is the man who could believe in both these kinds of proposals at once. For him witches, devils, angels, remarkable interventions of Providence, and the certainty of eternal judgment were as real as gravity. For his mind there was no contradiction between working for social justice and spending two or perhaps three days a week in secret fasts; no conflict between hailing Copernicus and Newton and preaching the imminence of the millennium, now that the seven last plagues of the Vial are about to be poured out on the Papal Empire; no conflict between studying the Talmud and preaching the Covenant of Grace.

Evaluation of Mather's literary achievement ought to profit from the same kind of attention to his prose style, which has too often been dismissed as fervid and pedantic. The remarkable quantity of his work, the cleanness of his manuscripts, and the testimony of his son all indicate that he wrote very rapidly, but the charge that his writing is fervid seems superficial. Although a small portion of his work fits the description, its importance has been exaggerated by the typographical devices used in his books and by the dubious belief that he was "neurotic" and therefore unable to control his rhetoric.

The prevalence of learned allusions and foreign quotations has also been exaggerated, partly because Mather defended these useful ornaments and partly because readers of his history of New England must traverse an unusually thick jungle of classical fact and lore, with a name dropping from every tree, before they can escape from his self-conscious introduction into the history itself. All this may be of little comfort to readers of *Bonifacius*, who will find that Mather studded some pages with what he liked to consider jewels of Latin and Greek. Those who are not completely antagonized may take some comfort in noting how aptly many of these come forth from the index of Mather's *Quotidiana* or the electronic computer of his extraordinary mind. Repeatedly, the quotation is apt, and Mather's comment repeatedly makes it so.

Notice, too, how much of the prose in *Bonifacius* is plain, forceful, precise. Mather's speed makes his paragraphs repetitious, and it is difficult for us to avoid overemphasizing his italics, but I am convinced that much of Mather's writing is plainer than any by Thomas Hooker or John Cotton. Even in *Bonifacius* this passage on brutal schoolmasters seems as representative as the more elaborate classical quotations:

Ajax Flagellifer may be read at the school. He is not fit for to be the master of it. Let it not be said of the scholars, "They are brought up *in the school of Tyrannus*." *Pliny* says, that *bears* are the fatter for beating. Fitter to have the conduct of *bears* than of ingenuous *boys*, are the masters, that can't give a *bit* of learning, but they must give a *knock* with it. Send 'em to be tutors of the famous *Lithuanian* school, at *Samourgan*. The harsh, fierce, *Orbilian* way of treating the children, too commonly used in the *school*, is a dreadful *curse* of God upon our miserable offspring, who are *born children of wrath*. It is boasted now and then of a *school-*

master, that such and such a *brave man* had his education under him. There is nothing said, how many that might have been *brave men*, have been destroyed by him; how many *brave wits*, have been dispirited, confounded, murdered, by his *barbarous* way of managing them.

Bonifacius is an important historical document because it brings to bear on the world of affairs all the piety and ingenuity that New England Puritanism had been nourishing, despite theological and political troubles, for eighty years. Without wavering from the central conviction of Puritans that man exists to glorify God, Cotton Mather exhorts all Christians to hunt opportunities to do good in the world. It is from this perspective, rather than by focusing on practical rewards, that we can best understand Puritan influences on Benjamin Franklin, later reformers, and American benevolence in the twentieth century. We continue to say, with the author of *Bonifacius*, that the ways of honest men are simple and the ways of the wicked are subtle, but we seek to devise a similar ingenuity for doing good around the world. We may also find it especially interesting that Mather the American, unlike his English predecessor Richard Baxter, says not a word about the danger that our efforts to do good may lead to disaster.

David Levin

NOTE ON THE TEXT

The first edition of *Bonifacius* was published, anonymously, in Boston, 1710. It had gone through eighteen editions by the time Thomas J. Holmes compiled his definitive bibliography of Mather's works in 1940. George Burder of London published a revised edition in 1807, and all subsequent editions before 1845 followed Burder's lamentable efforts to improve Mather's prose style. All these editions were published under the running title of the original, *Essays to Do Good*. In 1845, "an exact reprint" of the first edition was published in Boston by the Massachusetts Sabbath School Society.

The John Harvard Library edition follows the original text of 1710, which included the Appendix on Indian Christianity and the Advertisement for *Biblia Americana*. In certain matters of form, however, a few changes seem appropriate.

1. All words appear in modern American spelling rather than the English usage of Mather's time. Apostrophes thus give way to the letter "e" in such words as "employ'd" and the letter "u" disappears from "endeavour."

2. Initial capitals follow modern American usage. Because Mather places them not only on nouns but also on some verbs and adjectives, and in no discernible pattern, there seems to be no point in distracting the modern reader with them. A brief examination of Mather's manuscripts, moreover, will convince any reader that it is often difficult to be certain that Mather has indeed used an initial capital. Many of these in the published text may have been added by the printer.

3. Mather's italics present the same kind of problem, but I have reproduced them because they often serve a clear rhetorical purpose. At the beginning of his section on the family, for example, he says that every man should devise all the good "that may render his *relatives*, the better for him. One great way to prove ourselves *really good*, is to be *relatively good*." The pun

hardly deserves the emphatic attention that italics will give it for modern readers, but it seems to me wiser to caution readers against overstressing Mather's italics than to omit them altogether. In the long paragraph on gravity that I have quoted above, p. xxiv, the italics come directly from Mather's own manuscript, and some of them are rhetorically important. We should notice them without giving every italicized word the weight it would have in a modern text, and without requiring an apparent reason for every use of italics. Many italicized words will seem no more valuable than the initial capitals, but, with the single exception discussed in the next paragraph, I have refused to attempt the distinction, for fear of distorting his style.

4. The exception refers to obvious quotations. When certain that Mather or his printer uses italics to indicate a quotation, I have changed the passage to roman type and have indicated the quotation with modern quotation marks. I have therefore had to italicize in some of these quotations a word or two that in Mather's italicized version had been printed in roman for emphasis. When unsure of Mather's intention I have retained his italics.

5. Mather's square brackets—[ ]—have been changed to parentheses, except when they indicate his interpolations in quoted passages.

6. When Mather obviously uses a semicolon as we would use a colon, to introduce a quotation, I have used the colon. When his parenthetical phrasing calls for a comma, I have changed his semicolon to a comma.

7. Some of Mather's commas have also been deleted. I have tried, however, to reprint every comma that might serve a rhetorical purpose and every one (as in his very first sentence) that might render Mather's meaning ambiguous. I have tried to retain the rhythm of his prose, deleting commas before parentheses but retaining all those that might indicate a pause, however slight and however awkward.

Here, as with Mather's profusion of italics, we must choose between two kinds of distortion. By retaining almost all the commas, we run the risk of stressing pauses more heavily than Mather's contemporaries would have stressed them; but adopting modern usage would change his rhythm even more drastically. Mather was intensely interested in style; he punctuated rhetorically rather than grammatically, and somewhat more freely than a number of his contemporaries. It seems wise to reproduce a text that will enable students of style to gauge the meaning of his pauses.

8. The original edition uses two sizes of capitals, and Gothic type. All these appear in the John Harvard Library edition as large and small capitals, for it seems unnecessary to distinguish degrees of emphasis and printer's ornament for an audience so little accustomed to these devices.

9. The original edition was printed consecutively, with sections (§) numbered in arabic. I have reproduced these numbers but have also added chapter titles, in brackets, and a table of contents.

10. As footnotes I have provided rough translations of all those foreign phrases that Mather himself does not translate in the text.

My work on this edition began under a fellowship at the Center for Advanced Study in the Behavioral Sciences, to which I am grateful for the freedom to pursue a variety of interests and for the precise, sympathetic assistance of Mrs. Joan Warmbrunn. Bernard Bailyn corrected some serious errors and, along with Francelia Mason and Claude M. Simpson, gave me invaluable advice on the difficult problems of preparing a modern text. Thomas C. Moser's criticism improved the prose of the Introduction. A number of Mather's recondite allusions would remain unidentified if I had not had the resourceful help of librarians in the British Museum and at Stanford University. My greatest intellectual debt is to the late Perry Miller, for whom I present this edition as the tribute of a grateful student to the memory of a great teacher.

BONIFACIUS

AN ESSAY
Upon the GOOD, that is to be
DEVISED and DESIGNED,
BY THOSE
Who Desire to Answer the Great END
of *Life*, and to DO GOOD
While they *Live*.

A BOOK Offered,

First, in General, unto all CHRISTIANS;
in a PERSONAL Capacity, or in
a RELATIVE.
Then more Particularly,
Unto MAGISTRATES, unto MINISTERS,
unto PHYSICIANS, unto LAWYERS,
unto SCHOLEMASTERS, unto Wealthy
GENTLEMEN, unto several Sorts of
OFFICERS, unto CHURCHES, and
unto all SOCIETIES of a Religious
Character and Intention. With Humble
PROPOSALS, of Unexceptionable
METHODS, to *Do Good* in the World.

Eph. VI:18. *Knowing that whatsoever good thing any
man does, the same shall he receive of the Lord.*

BOSTON in *N. England:* Printed by *B. Green,* for
Samuel Gerrish at his Shop in Corn Hill. 1710.

I

THE PREFACE

Among the many *customs* of the world, which 'tis become almost *necessary* to comply withal, it seems, this is one, *that a book must not appear without a Preface.* And this little book willingly submits unto the *customary ceremony.* It comes with a *Preface;* however it shall not be one like the Gates of *Mindus.*[1] But there appears a greater difficulty in a compliance with another usage: that of, *an Epistle Dedicatory. Dedications* are become such foolish and fulsome *adulations,* that they are now in a manner *useless.* Oftentimes all the use of them is, to furnish the critics on, *The Manners of the Age,* with matter of ridicule. The excellent *Boyle*[2] employed but a just expression, in saying: "'Tis almost as much out of fashion in such addresses to omit giving praises [I may say, *unjust* ones] as 'tis to believe the praises given on such an occasion." Sometimes the authors themselves live to *see* their *own* mistakes, and *own* them. An *Austin*[3] makes the flourishes, he has once used in a *Dedication,* an article of his *Retractations;* a *Calvin* does revoke a *Dedication,* because he finds he had made it unto an unworthy person. I may add, that at other times, everyone sees, what the authors would be at, and how much they *write for themselves* when they flatter other men. Another course must now be steered.

If a book of ESSAYS TO DO GOOD were to be dedicated unto a person of quality, it ought to seek a patron, who is a true *man of honor,* and of uncommon *goodness.* Thy patron, O

3

book of *benefits* to the world, should be, a general and most generous *benefactor* to mankind; one, who never counts himself so well *advanced*, as in *stooping* to *do good*, unto all that may be the *better* for him; one whose *highest ambition* is to abound in *serviceable condescensions:* a stranger to the *gain of oppression;* the common *refuge* of the oppressed, and the distressed; one who will know nothing that is *base;* a lover of all *good men*, in all persuasions; able to *distinguish* them, and loving them without any *distinction*. Let him also be one, who has nobly stripped himself of *emoluments* and *advantages*, when they would have encumbered his opportunities, to serve his nation. Yea, presume upon one, who has governed and adorned the greatest and bravest city on the face of the earth, and so much the *delight* of that city, as well as of the rest of *mankind*, that she shall never count her honor or welfare more consulted, than when he appears for her as a *representative*, in the most illustrious of all the assemblies in the world: beloved by the *Queen of Cities*, the fairest and richest Lady of the Universe.

In one word, A PUBLIC SPIRIT. Let him THEREFORE, and upon more than all these accounts be, Sir WILLIAM ASHURST. For as of old the poet observed, upon mentioning the name of *Plutarch*, the *echo* answered, "Philosophy": so now, "A PUBLIC SPIRIT" will immediately be the *echo* and reply, in the sense of all men, and with a repetition oftener than that at *Pont-Chareton* [Charenton-le Pont?], if the name of Sir WILLIAM ASHURST [4] once be mentioned. HE 'tis whom the confession of *all men* brings into the catalogue, with *Abraham*, and *Joseph*, and those other ancient blessings, who are thus excellently described by *Grotius:* [5] "*Homines demerendis hominibus nati, qui omnem beneficii collocandi occasionem ponebant in lucro.*" *
America afar off also knows him; the *American* colonies have their eye upon the efforts of his *goodness* for them. *Norunt, et*

* Men born to serve mankind, who consider profitable every opportunity to do good.

4

Antipodes.† Nations of Christianized *Indians* likewise pray for him, as their GOVERNOR. To *him,* the design of such a book will be acceptable; whatever may be the poor and mean way of treating the *noble subject,* which it would insist upon. To *him* it wishes that all the blessings of those who *devise good,* may be forever multiplied.

I will presume to do something, that will carry a sweet harmony, with one of the main methods to be observed in prosecuting the design of this book; which is, for *brethren to dwell together in unity,* and carry on every good design with *united endeavors.*—

They will pardon me, if I take the leave to join with him, in the testimonies of our great esteem, for an honorable disposition to *love good men,* and to *do good in the world,* his excellent brother-in-law. The well-known name of a JOSEPH THOMPSON has long been valued, and shall always be remembered, in the country where this book is published. God will be glorified, for the piety which adorns him, and the *pure religion,* which in the midst of the world, and of temptations from it, keeps him so *unspotted from the world.* It was the maxim of a pagan *Asdrubal* in *Livy,* "*Raro simul hominibus, bona fortuna, bonaque mens datur.*" ‡ *Christianity* will, in this gentleman, give to the world, an happy experiment,[6] that the maxim is capable of a confutation. Because a book of *Essays to Do Good* will doubtless find its agreeable acceptance with one of so *good a mind,* and the Treasurer of a corporation formed on the intention to do in *America* that good which is of all the greatest, whereof Sir *William Ashurst* is the Governor, he also has a part in the humble tender of it; and it must wish unto him *all the blessings of goodness.*

The BOOK requires that now some account be given of it. It was a passage, in a speech of an envoy from His *Britannic*

† Even the antipodes know.
‡ Seldom are prosperity and a good heart given to men at the same time.

Majesty, to the Duke of *Brandenburg* twenty years ago: "A capacity to do good, not only gives a title to it, but also makes the doing of it a duty." *Ink* were too vile a liquor to write that passage. *Letters of gold* were too mean, to be the preservers of it. Paper of *amyanthus* would not be precious and perennous enough, to perpetuate it.

To be brief, Reader, the *book* now in thy hands, is nothing but an illustration, and a prosecution of that memorable sentence. As *gold* is capable of a wonderful dilatation—experiment has told us, it may be so dilated, that the hundred-thousandth part of a *grain*, may be visible without a *microscope*—this *golden sentence* may be as much extended; no man can say how much. This book is but a *beating* upon it. And at the same time, 'tis a commentary on that inspired maxim, Gal. 6. 10: "As we have opportunity, let us do good unto all men." Every PROPOSAL here made upon it hopes to be able to say, "When I am tried, I shall come forth as gold."

I have not been left altogether uninformed, that all the rules of *discretion* and *behavior*, are embryoed in that one word, MODESTY. But it will be no breach of *modesty*, to be very *positive* in asserting, that the only *wisdom* of man lies in conversing with the great GOD, and His glorious CHRIST; and in engaging as many others as we can, to join with us in this our blessedness; thereby promoting His *Kingdom* among the children of men; and in studying to *do good* unto all about us; to be *blessings* in our several relations; to heal the disorders, and help the distresses of a miserable world, as far as ever we can extend our influences. It will be no trespass upon the rules of *modesty*, with all possible *assurance* to assert, that no man begins to be *wise*, till he come to make this the *main* purpose and pleasure of his life; yea, that every man will at some time or other be so *wise* as to own, that everything without this is but *folly*, tho' alas, the most of men come not unto it, until it be *too late*.

Millions of men, in all ranks, besides those whose *dying* thoughts are collected in, *The Fair Warnings to a Careless World*, have at length declared their conviction of it. It will be no *immodesty* in me to say: The man who is not satisfied of the *wisdom* in making it the work of his *life* to *do good*, is always to be beheld with the pity due to an *idiot*. No *first principles* are more *peremptorily* to be adhered unto. Or, do but grant *a judgment to come*, and my assertion is presently victorious.

I will not be *immodest*, and yet I will boldly say: The man is worse than a *pagan*, who will not come into this notion of things, *Vir bonus est commune bonum;* § and *Vivit is qui multis est usui;* and *Utilitate hominum, nil debet esse homini antiquius.* None but a *good man*, is really a *living* man; and the more *good* any man does, the more he really *lives. All the rest is death;* or belongs to it. Yea, you must excuse me, if I say: The *Mahometan* also shall condemn the man, who comes not into the principles of this book. For I think, it occurs no less than three times in the *Alcoran: God loves those that are inclined to do good.*

For this *way of living*, if we are fallen into a *generation*, wherein men will cry, "*(Sotah!)* He's a fool" of him that practices it, as the rabbis foretell, 'twill be in the *generation wherein the Messiah comes;* yet there will be a *wiser* generation, and *Wisdom will be justified of her children.* Among the Jews, there has been an *Ezra*, whose *head* they called, *the throne of wisdom:* Among the *Greeks* there has been a *Democritus*, who was called Σοφια,‖ in the abstract; the later ages knew a *Gildas*, who wore the surname of *Sapiens;* but it is the man whose *temper* and *intent* it is, *to do good*, that is the truly *wise man* after all.[7] And indeed had a man the hands of a *Briareus*,[8] they would all be too few to *do good;* he might

§ A good man is a public blessing [or, a common good].
‖ Wisdom.

7

find occasions to call for more than all of them. The English nation once had a sect of men called *bon-hommes*, or *good men*. The ambition of this book, is to revive and enlarge a *sect* that may claim that name; yea, to solicit, that it may extend beyond the bounds of a *sect*, by the coming of *all men* into it.

Of all the *trees in the garden of God;* which is there, that envies not the *palm-tree*, out of which alone *Plutarch* tells us, the *Babylonians* fetched more than three hundred commodities? Or the *cocoa-tree*, so beneficial to man, that a vessel may be built, and rigged, and freighted and victualled from that alone? To *plant* such *trees of righteousness*, and *prune* them, is the hope of the book now before us.

The men who *devise good*, will now give me leave to mind them of some things, by which they may be a little fortified for their grand intention; for, Sirs, you are to pass between *Bozez* (or, Dirty) and *Seneh* (or, Thorny),[9] and encounter an host of things worse than *Philistines*, in your undertaking.

MISCONSTRUCTION is one thing against which you will do well to furnish yourselves with the armor both of *prudence* and of *patience; prudence* for the preventing of it, *patience* for the enduring of it. You will unavoidably be put upon the doing of many *good things*, which other people will see but at a *distance*, and be unacquainted with the *motives* and *methods* of your doing them; yea, they may imagine their own *purposes* crossed, or clogged in what you do; and this will expose you to their censures. Yet more particularly; in your *essays to do good*, you may happen to be concerned with persons, whose *power* is greater than their *virtue*. It may be *needful* as well as *lawful*, for you, to mollify them, with acknowledgments of those things in them which may render them *honorable* or *considerable*, and forbear to take notice at the present, of what may be *culpable*. In this, you may aim at nothing under Heaven, but only, that you may be the more able to *do good* unto *them;* or by *them* to *do good* unto others. And yet, if you are not very wary, this your *civility* may prove your *disadvantage:* especially, if you find yourselves obliged, either to change your *opinion* of the persons, or to tax any *miscarriage* in them. The injustice of the censures upon you may be much, as if *Paul* rebuking *Felix* [10] for his *unrighteousness* and *unchastity*, should have been twitted with it, as an *inconstancy*, an *inconsistency*, in that very lately he had complimented this very *Felix*, and said he was very glad he had one of such abilities and accomplishments to be concerned withal, and one so well acquainted with the affairs of his nation. But you must not be *uneasy*, if you should be thus unjustly dealt withal. *Jerome* [11] had written highly, of *Origen*, as a man of bright endowments; anon he wrote as hardly against some things that *Origen* was (it may be, wrongfully) accused of. They cried out upon *Jerome* for his *levity*, yea, *falsity*. He despised the calumny, and replied: "I did once commend, what I thought was great in him, and now condemn what I find to be evil in him." I pray, where's the contradiction! I say, be cautious; but I say again, be not *uneasy*.

What I add unto it, is: that you must be above all DISCOURAGEMENTS. Look for them, and with a magnanimous *courage* overlook them.

Some have observed, that the most *concealed*, and yet the most *violent*, of all our *passions*, usually is that of IDLENESS. It lays *adamantine chains* of death and of darkness upon us. It holds in *chains* that cannot be shaken off, all our other, though never so impetuous inclinations. That no more *hurt* is done in the world, is very much owing to a sort of *scorbutic* and *spontaneous* lassitude on the minds of men, as well as that no more *good* is done. A *Pharaoh* will do us no wrong if he tell us, "Ye are idle, ye are idle." We have usually more *strength* to *do good*, than we have *will* to lay it out. Sirs, *Be up, and be doing!* 'Tis too soon yet sure for an *Hic situs est.*¶

¶ This is the place [to rest].

If you meet with vile INGRATITUDE from those whom you have laid under the most *weighty obligations*, don't wonder at it. Such a *turpitude* is the nature of man sunk into, that men had rather bear any *weight* than that of *obligations*. They will own small ones; but return wonderful hatred and malice for such as are extraordinary. They will render it a *dangerous* thing, to be very *charitable* and *beneficent*. *Communities* will do it as well as *individuals*. *Excess* of *desert* at length turns into a kind of *demerit*. Men will sooner forgive great *injuries*, than great *services*. He that built a matchless castle for the *Poles*, for his *reward*, had his *eyes put out*, that he might not build such another. Such things are enough to make one *sick of the world*; but, my friend, they should not make thee *sick* of *essays to do good in the world*. A *conformity* to thy Saviour, and a *communion* with Him, let that carry thee through all!

'Twill be impossible to avoid ENVY. For a *right work*, and for a *good* one, and especially, if a man do *many* such, he shall be *envied of his neighbor*. 'Tis incredible, the force that the *pride* of men, has to produce *detraction! Pride*, working in a sort of *impatience*, that any man should be, or do more than they. The minds of men, as one says, "have got the vapors; a sweet report of anyone throws them into convulsions and agonies; a foul one refreshes 'em." You must bear all the *outrage* of it; and there is but one sort of *revenge* to be allowed you. One says, "There is not any revenge more heroic, than that which torments envy by doing of good."

It is a surprising passage, which a late *French* author has given us: "That a man of *good merit*, is a kind of *public enemy*. And that by *engrossing* a great many applauses, which would serve to gratify a great many others, he cannot but be *envied;* and that men do naturally *hate*, what they *esteem* very much, but cannot *love*." But, my readers, let us not be surprised at it. You have read, who suffered the *ostracisms* at *Athens;* and what a pretty reason the country fellow had, why he gave his voice, for the banishing of *Aristides* (because he was everywhere always called, *the Just*): and for what reason the *Ephori* laid a mulct upon *Agesilaus* (because he did above other men possess the hearts of the Lacedæmonians).[12] You have read, the reason why the *Ephesians* expelled the best of their citizens (*Nemo de nobis unus excellat; sed si quis extiterit, alio in loco, et apud alios sit*): If any will outdo their neighbors, let 'em find another place to do it. You have read, that he who conquered *Hannibal*, saw it necessary to retire from *Rome*, that the merit of others might have more notice taken of it. My authors tell me, "At all times, nothing has been more dangerous among men than too shining a merit." But, my readers, the terror of this *envy* must not intimidate you. I must press you, to *do good*, and be so far from *affrighted* at, that you shall rather be generously *delighted* in, the most envious *deplumations*.

I wish I may prove a *false prophet*, when I foretell you one *discouragement* more, which you will have to conflict withal. DERISION is what I mean. And let not my *prediction* be derided, I pray. It was long since noted, *Ridiculum acri fortius et melius magnas plerumque sicat res.** It is a thing of late started, that the way of *banter*, and *scoffing*, and *ridicule*, or, the *Bart'lemew-Fair method*,[13] as they please to call it, is a more effectual way to discourage all *goodness*, and put it out of countenance, than *fire* and *faggot*. No *cruelties* are so insupportable to humanity, as *cruel mockings*. It is extremely probable, that the *Devil* being somewhat *chained* up in several places, from the other ways of *persecution*, will more than ever apply himself to *this*. *Essays to do good* shall be derided, with all the *art* and *wit*, that he can inspire into his *Janizaries* (a *Yani-cheer*,[14] or *a new order*, the Grand Seigneur of Hell has instituted). Exquisite *profaneness* and *buffoonery* shall try their skill to laugh people out of them. The men who abound

* Ridicule often cuts most effectively.

in them shall be exposed on the *stage; libels*, and *lampoons*, and *satires*, the most poignant that ever were invented, shall be darted at them; and *pamphlets* full of lying stories, be scattered, with a design to make them *ridiculous. Hic se aperit Diabolus!* † The *Devil* will try, whether the *fear of being laughed at*, will not cool and scare, a *zeal to do good*, out of the world.—*Sed tu contra audentior ito.*‡ Sirs, *despise the shame*, whatever *contradiction of sinners* you meet withal; you know, what Example did so before you. *Quit you like men, be strong;* you know who gives you the direction. Say with resolution, "The proud have had me greatly in derision, yet have not I declined to do as much good as I could." If you should arrive to a share in such sufferings, I will humbly *show you mine opinion*, about the best conduct under them; 'tis *neglect*, and *contempt*. I have a whole university on my side. The University of *Helmstadt*, upon a late abuse offered unto it, had this noble passage in a declaration: *Visum fuit, non alio remedio, quam generoso silentio, et pio contemptu, utendum nobis esse.*§ Go on to *do good;* and *go well, comely in your going,* like the noble creature, which *turneth not away for any.* A life spent in industrious *essays to do good*, will be your powerful, and perpetual vindication. 'Twill give you such a *well-established interest* in the minds where *conscience* is advised withal, that a few squibbing, silly, impotent allatrations [15] will never be able to extinguish it. If they go to ridicule you in their printed excursions, your name will be so *oiled*, no ink will stick upon it. I remember, *Valerianus Magnus* [16] being abused by a *Jesuit*, who had labored (by a *modest inquiry*, you may be sure!) to make him ridiculous, made no other defense, but only on every stroke adjoined, *"Mentiris impudentissime. It is a most impudent lie, Sir!"* And such an answer might very

† The Devil appears here.
‡ But you must be more daring against him.
§ We ought to use no other remedy than a generous silence and a pious contempt.

truly be given, to every line of some stories that I have seen elsewhere *brewed* by another, who is *no Jesuit*.[17] But even *so much answer* to their *folly*, is *too much notice* of it. It is well observed, "The contempt of such discourses discredits them, and takes away the pleasure from those that make them." And it is another observation, *That when they of whom we have heard very ill, yet are found by us upon trial to be very good, we naturally conclude, they have a merit that is troublesome to some other people.* The rule then is, *Be* very *good*, yea, *Do* very much *good*; and cast a generous *disdain* upon *contumelies*; the *great remedy* against them. If you want a pattern I can give you an imperial one; it was a *Vespasian*, who when one spoke ill of him, said, "*Ego, cum nihil faciam dignum propter quod contumelia afficiar, mendacia nihil curo.*" ‖ And I am deceived, if it be not an easy thing to be as honest a man as a Vespasian! [18]

Sirs, an unfainting resolution to *do good*, and an *unwearied well-doing*, is the thing, that is now urged upon you. And may this little *book* now be so happy, as herein to do the part of a *monitor*, unto the readers of it.

I don't find that I have spent so many weeks in composing the book, as *Descartes*, though a profound *geometrician*, declares he spent in studying the solution of one *geometrical question*. Yet the composure is grown beyond what I desired it should have done; and there is not one *proposal* in it, but what well pursued, would yield the mind a more solid and lasting satisfaction, than the solution of all the *problems* in *Euclid*, or in *Pappus*.[19] 'Tis a vanity in writers, to compliment the readers, with a, "Sorry 'tis no better." Instead of *that*, I freely tell my readers: I have written what is not unworthy of their perusal. If I did not think so, truly, I would not publish it. For no man living has demanded it of me; 'tis not published, "to gratify the

‖ While [that is, *so long as*] I do nothing to deserve the abuse with which I am afflicted, I don't worry about the lies.

importunity of friends," as your authors use to trifle; but it is to *use an importunity with others,* in a point, on which I thought they wanted it. And I will venture to say, There is not one *whimsy* in all my *proposals.* I propose nothing, but what the *conscience* of every good man will say, "It were well, if it could be accomplished." That writer was in the right of it, who says, "I can't understand, how any honest man can print a book, and yet profess, that he thinks none will be the wiser or better for the reading of it." Indeed, I own that my subject is worthy to be much *better* handled, and my manner of handling it is not such that I dare do as the famous painter *Titian* did on his pieces, write my name, with a double, *Fecit, Fecit,* as much as to say, "Very well done": and I must have utterly suppressed it, if I had been of the same humor, with *Cimabue,* another famous painter, who, if himself or any other spied the least fault in his pieces, would utterly deface them and destroy them, though he had bestowed a twelvemonth's pains upon them. Yet I will venture to say, the book is full of *reasonable* and *serviceable* things; and it would be well for us, if such things were hearkened to; and I have *done well* to offer them.

Who is the author, there is no need of inquiring. This will be unavoidably known in the vicinity. But his writing *without* a name (as well as *not for one*), will conceal it from the most of those to whom the book may come. And the concealment of his name, he apprehends, may be of some use to the book; for now, not *who,* but *what,* is the only thing to be considered.

It was a vanity in one author, and there may be too many guilty of the like, to demand, *Ubi mea legis, me agnosce.* In true unblushing English, *Reader, whatever you do, count the author somebody.* But, I pray, Sir, what are *you,* that mankind should be at all concerned about you? He was almost as great a man, as any ecclesiastical preferments could make him, who

14

yet would not have so much as his name in his epitaph; he would only have, *Hic jacet, umbra, cinis, nihil.*¶ There shall be no other name on this composure; *hic scribit (vel Scripturire studet et audet) umbra, cinis, nihil.**

However, he is very strongly persuaded, there is a day very near at hand, when books of such a tendency as this, will be the most welcome things imaginable, to many thousands of readers, and have more than one edition. Yea, *great will be the army of them that publish them!* M.DCC.XVI. is a-coming.²⁰

A vast variety of *new ways to do good* will be lit upon; *paths* which no fowl of the best flight at noble designs has yet *known;* and which the *vulture's* most piercing eye has not yet seen, and where the *lions* of the strongest resolution have never passed.

In the meantime, North Britain will be *distinguished* (pardon me, if I use the term, *Goshenized*) ²¹ by irradiations from Heaven upon it, of such a tendency. There will be found a set of excellent men, in that Reformed and Renowned Church of *Scotland,* with whom the most refined and extensive essays to *do good* will become so natural that the whole world will fare the better for them. To these, this Book is humbly presented, by a great admirer of the *good things* daily doing among them; as knowing, that if nowhere else, yet among *them,* it will find some reception; they will *not be forgetful to entertain* such a *stranger!*—

The censure of *writing too much* (no, though he should go as far as *Terentianus Carthaginensis* tells us *Varro* did) he counts not worth answering. —And, I pray, why not also *preaching too much!* —But *Erasmus,* who wrote more, has furnished him with an answer, which is all that ever he intends to give unto

¶ Here lies a shadow, ashes, nothing.

* Here writes (or tries and dares to write) a shadow, ashes, nothing.

it: *Accusant quod nimium fecerim; conscientia mea me accusat, quod minus fecerim, quodque lentior fuerim.* In plain ingenuous English: "The *censure* of others upbraids me, that I have done so *much;* my own *conscience* condemns me that I have done so *little*." The good God forgive my *slothfulness!* [22]

[CHAPTER ONE:] ESSAYS TO DO GOOD

SUCH *glorious things are spoken* in the oracles of our good God, concerning them who *devise good*, that A BOOK OF GOOD DEVICES may very reasonably demand attention and acceptance from them that have any impressions of the most *reasonable religion* upon them. I am *devising* such a BOOK; but at the same time offering a sorrowful demonstration, that if men would set themselves to *devise good*, a world of *good* might be done, more than there is, in this *present evil world*. It is very sure, the world has *need enough*. There needs abundance to be done, that the great GOD and His CHRIST may be more known and served in the world; and that the *errors* which are *impediments* to the *acknowledgments* wherewith men ought to glorify their Creator and Redeemer, may be rectified. There needs abundance to be done, that the *evil manners* of the world, by which men are *drowned in perdition*, may be reformed; and mankind rescued from the epidemical corruption and slavery which has overwhelmed it. There needs abundance to be done, that the *miseries* of the world may have *remedies* and *abatements* provided for them; and that miserable people may be relieved and comforted. The world has according to the computation of some, above seven hundred millions of people now living in it. What an ample field among all these, to *do good* upon! In a word, *the kingdom of God* in the world calls for innumerable *services* from us. To do SUCH THINGS is to DO GOOD. Those men DEVISE GOOD, who shape any DEVICES to do things of such a tendency; whether the things be of a *spiritual* importance, or of a *temporal*. You see, Sirs, the general matter, appearing as yet but as a *chaos*, which is to be wrought upon. *Oh! that the good Spirit of God may*

17

now fall upon us, and carry on the glorious work which lies before us!

§2. 'Tis to be supposed, my readers will readily grant, that it is an excellent, a virtuous, a laudable thing to be full of *devices*, to bring about such *noble purposes*. For any man to deride, or to despise my proposal, *that we resolve and study to do as much good in the world as we can*, would be so black a character, that I am not willing to make a supposal of it in any of those with when [1] I am concerned. Let no man pretend unto the name of *a Christian*, who does not approve the proposal of *a perpetual endeavor to do good in the world*. What pretension can such a man have to be *a follower of the Good One?* The primitive *Christians* gladly accepted and improved the name, when the pagans by a mistake styled them, *Chrestians;* because it signified, *useful ones*. The *Christians* who have no ambition to be so, shall be condemned by the pagans, among whom it was a term of the highest honor, to be termed, *a benefactor;* to have *done good*, was accounted *honorable*. The philosopher being asked why everyone desired so much to look upon a fair object, he answered, that *it was a question of a blind man*. If any man ask, as wanting the sense of it, "What is it worth the while to *do good* in the world?," I must say, "It sounds not like the question of a good man." The Αισθησις πνευματικη, as *Origen* calls it, the *spiritual taste* of every good man will make him have an unspeakable *relish* for it. Yea, unworthy to be discoursed as a *man*, is he, who is not for *doing of good among men*. An *enemy* to the proposal, *that mankind may be the better for us*, deserves to be reckoned, little better than, *a common enemy of mankind*. How cogently do I bespeak, a good reception of what is now designed! I produce not only *religion*, but even *humanity* itself, as full of a *fiery indignation against the adversaries of the design*. Excuse me, Sirs; I declare, that if I could have my choice, I would never *eat* or *drink*, or *walk*, with such an one as long as I live; or, look on him as any other than one by whom *humanity* itself is debased and blemished. A very *wicked writer*, has yet found himself compelled by the force of *reason*, to publish this confession. "To love the public, to study an universal good, and to promote the interest of the whole world, as far as is in our power, is surely the highest of goodness, and makes that temper, which we call Divine." And, he goes on: "Is the doing of good for glory's sake so divine a thing? [Alas, too much *humane*, Sir!] Or, is it not a diviner to do good, even where it may be thought inglorious? Even unto the ungrateful, and unto those who are wholly insensible of the good they receive!" A man must be far gone in *wickedness*, who will open his mouth, against such *maxims* and *actions!* A better pen has remarked it; yea, the man must be much a stranger in history, who has not made the remark. *To speak truth, and to do good, were in the esteem even of the heathen world, most God-like qualities*. God forbid, that in the esteem of the *Christian world* for those qualities, there should be any abatement!

§3. I won't yet propose the *reward* of *well-doing*, and the glorious things which the *mercy* and *truth* of God will do, for them who *devise good*, because I would have to do with such, as will esteem it, a sufficient *Reward* unto itself. I will imagine that generous ingenuity, in my readers, which will dispose them to count themselves *well-rewarded* in the thing itself, if God will accept them to *do good* in the world. It is an invaluable *honor*, to *do good;* it is an incomparable *pleasure*. A man must look upon himself as *dignified* and *gratified* by GOD, when an *opportunity* to *do good* is put into his hands. He must embrace it with *rapture*, as enabling him directly to answer the great END of his being. He must manage it with *rapturous delight*, as a most suitable business, as a most precious privilege. He must *sing in those ways of the Lord*, wherein he cannot but find himself, while he is *doing of good*. As the saint of old sweetly sang, "I was glad, when they said unto me, Let us go into the House of the Lord." ² Thus ought we to be *glad*, when any *opportunity* to *do good,* is offered unto us. We should need no *arguments,* to make us entertain the offer; but we should *naturally* fly into the matter, as most agreeable to the *divine nature* whereof we are *made partakers.* It should *oblige* us wonderfully! An ingot of gold presented unto us, not more obliging! Think, Sirs, *Now I enjoy what I am for! Now I attain what I wish for!* Some servants of God have been so strongly disposed this way, that they have cheerfully made a tender of any *recompense* that could be desired (yea, rather than fail, a *pecuniary* one) unto any friend that would *think* for them, and *supply* the *barrenness* of their thoughts, and *suggest* unto them any special and proper *methods,* wherein they may be *serviceable.* Certainly, to *do good,* is a thing that brings its own *recompense,* in the opinion of those, who reckon a kind *information* of a point wherein they may *do good,* worthy to be by them requited with a *recompense* to the *informer.* I will only say: "If any of you are strangers unto such a disposition as this, to look upon an *opportunity* to *do good,* as a thing that *enriches* you, and to look upon yourselves as *enriched,* and *favored* of God, when He does employ you to *do good:* I have done with you." I would pray them, to lay the *book* aside; it will disdain to carry on any further conversation with 'em! It handles a subject on which the wretches of the house of *Caleb,*³ will not be conversed withal. It is content with one of Dr. *Stoughton's* Introductions: "It is enough to me, that I speak to wise men, whose reason shall be my rhetoric, to Christians, whose conscience shall be my eloquence." ⁴

§4. Though the assertion fly never so much like a *chainshot* among us, and rake down all before it, I will again, and again assert it; *that we might every one of us do more good than we do.* And therefore, this is the FIRST PROPOSAL, to be made unto us: *to be exceedingly humbled, that we have done so little good in the world.* I am not *uncharitable,* in saying: I know

not that *assembly* of Christians upon earth, which ought not to
be a *Bochim*,[5] in this consideration. Oh! tell me, what *Utopia*
I shall find it in! Sirs, let us begin to bring forth some *good
fruit*, by lamenting our own *great unfruitfulness*. Verily, *sins
of omission* must be confessed and bewailed; else we add unto
the number of them. The most *useful* men in the world, have
gone out of it, crying to God, "Lord, let my sins of omission be
forgiven to me!" Men that have made more than ordinary conscience about well-spending of their *time*, have had their death-
bed made uneasy by this reflection: *The loss of time now sits
heavy upon me.* Be sure, all *unregenerate* persons are, as our
Bible has told us, *unprofitable* persons. 'Tis not for nothing,
that the comparison of *thorns*, and *briars*, has been used, to
teach us, what they are. An unrenewed sinner, alas, he never
did *one good work* in all his *life!* In all his *life*, did I say? You
must give me that word again! He is *dead* while he *lives;* he is
dead in sins; he has never yet begun to *live unto God:* and, as
is he, so are *all the works of his hands;* they are *dead works.*
Ah! wretched *good-for-nothing.* Wonder, wonder at the
patience of Heaven, which yet forbears *cutting down* such a
cumberer of the ground. The best, and the first advice, to be
given unto such persons, is, *immediately to do their best, that
they may get out of their woeful unregeneracy.* Let them
immediately acknowledge the *necessity* of their turning to
God, but how *unable* they are to do it, and how *unworthy* that
God should make them *able. Immediately* let them lift up their
cry unto sovereign *grace*, to *quicken* them; and let them then
try, whether they cannot with *quickened* Souls, *plead* the
sacrifice and *righteousness* of a glorious CHRIST for their happy
reconciliation to God; seriously resolve upon a life of *obedience* to God, and *serious religion;* and resign themselves up
unto the *Holy Spirit*, that He may possess them, instruct them,
strengthen them, and *for His name's sake lead them in the paths
of holiness.* There will no *good* be done, till this be done. The

very *first-born* of all *devices* to *do good*, is in being *born again*, and in *devising means, that a banished* soul may no longer be *expelled* from the presence of God. But you that have been brought home to God, have sad cause, not only to deplore the *dark days* of your unregeneracy, wherein you did none but the *unfruitful works of darkness;* but also, that you have done so *little,* since God has quickened you and enabled you, to *do,* the things that should be done. How little, how little have you lived up, to the strains of *gratitude,* which might have been justly expected, since God has brought you *into His marvellous light!* The best of us may mourn in our complaint: "Lord, how little good have I done, to what I might have done!" Let the sense of this cause us to *loathe* and *judge* ourselves before the Lord: let it fill us with shame, and abase us wonderfully! How can we do any other, than with *David,* even make a cauldron of our couch, and a bath of our tears, when we consider how little *good* we have done! *Oh! that our heads were waters,* because they have been so *dry* of all thoughts to *do good! Oh! that our eyes were a fountain of tears,* because they have been so little upon the *lookout* for objects and methods to *do good* upon! For the *pardon* of this *evil-doing,* let us fly to the Great *Sacrifice,* which is our only *expiation.* Plead the *blood* of that *Lamb of God,* whose universal *usefulness* is one of those admirable properties, for which He has been called, *a lamb.* The *pardon* of our *barrenness* at *good works* being thus obtained, by faith in that *blood which cleanses from all sin,* that is the way for us to be rescued from a condemnation to *perpetual barrenness.* The dreadful sentence of, *Let no fruit grow on thee forever!* will be reversed and prevented, by such a *pardon.* Sirs, a true, right, evangelical procedure to *do good,* must have this *repentance* laid in the foundation of it! We do not *handle the matter wisely,* if a *foundation* be not laid thus *low,* and in the deepest *self-abasement.*

§5. How full, how full of *devices* are we, for our own *secular*

22

advantage! And how *expert* in *devising* many *little things,* to be done for ourselves! We apply our thoughts, with a mighty assiduity, unto the old question, *What shall I eat and drink, and wherewithal shall I be clothed?* It is with a very strong application of our thoughts, that we study, what we shall do for ourselves, in our *marriages,* in our *voyages,* in our *bargains,* and in many, many other concerns, wherein we are solicitous to have our condition easy. We solicitously *contrive,* that we may accomplish *good bargains,* and that we may steer clear of ten thousand *inconveniences,* to which, without some *contrivance,* we may lie obnoxious. The *business* of our *personal callings* we carry on with numberless thoughts, how we may *do well,* in what is to be done. To accomplish our temporal *business,* in affairs that cannot be numbered, we *find out witty inventions.* But, O rational, immortal, Heaven-born SOUL, are thy wonderous faculties capable of no greater improvements, no better employments? Why should a *soul* of such high capacities, a *soul* that may arrive to be clothed in the bright *scarlet* of *angels,* yet *embrace a dunghill!* O let a *blush* coloring beyond *scarlet,* be thy clothing for thy being found so meanly occupied! Alas, *in the multitude of thy thoughts within thee,* hast thou no dispositions to raise thy soul, unto some thoughts, *what may be done for* GOD, *and* CHRIST, *and for my own* SOUL, *and for the most considerable interests?* How many hundreds of *thoughts* have we, how to obtain or secure some trifle for ourselves; to *one,* how we may serve the interests of the glorious LORD, and of His people in the world? How can we now pretend, that we *love Him,* or, that a carnal, and criminal *self-love,* has not the dominion over us? I again come in, upon a *soul* of an Heavenly extract, and *smite* it, as the angel did the sleeping prisoner: *Awake, shake off thy shackles, lie no longer fettered in a base confinement unto nothing but a meaner sort of business.* Assume and assert the liberty of now and then thinking on the *noblest question* in the world: *What good may*

23

I do in the world? There was a time, when it was complained by no less a man, than *Gregory* the Great (the Bishop of *Rome*): *I am sunk into the world!* It may be the complaint of a *soul*, that minds all other things, and rarely calls to mind that *noblest question. Ah! star, fallen from Heaven,* and choked in dust, rise and soar up to something answerable to thy original. Begin a *course of thoughts,* which when begun, will be like a *resurrection from the dead.* They *which dwell in the dust, wake and sing,* and little anticipate the *life* which we are to live at the *resurrection of the dead,* when they livelily set themselves to think: *How may I be a blessing in the world?* And, *What may I do, that righteousness may more dwell in the world?*

§6. How much *hurt* may be done by *one wicked man?* Yea, sometimes *one wicked man,* of but small abilities, becoming an *indefatigable tool of the Devil,* may do an incredible deal of mischief in the world. We have seen some wretched instruments of *cursed memory,* ply the intention of *doing mischief,* at a strange rate; until they have undone a whole country; yea, unto the undoing of more than three kingdoms. 'Tis a melancholy consideration, which I am now upon: and I may say, an astonishing one! You will hardly find *one of a thousand,* who does near so much, to serve God and Christ, and his own soul, as you may see done by thousands to serve the Devil. *An horrible thing!*

"O my soul; thy *Maker,* and thy *Saviour,* so worthy of thy love, and thy all! A Lord, whose infinite goodness, will follow all that thou doest for Him, with remunerations, beyond all apprehension glorious! How little, how little, is it that thou doest for Him! At the same time, look into thy neighborhood; see there a monster of wickedness, who to his uttermost will serve a Devil, that will prove a *destroyer* unto him, and all whose *wages* will be *torments.* He *studies* how to serve the *Devil;* he is never weary of his *drudgery;* he racks his *invention* to go through with it. He *shames* me, he *shames* me won-

24

derfully! *O my God, I am ashamed, and blush to lift up my face unto thee, my God.*"

There is a man, of whom we read: "He deviseth mischief upon his bed, he sets himself in a way that is not good." Now, I beseech you, why should not we be as *active*, as *frequent*, as *forward*, in *devising of good;* and as full of *exquisite contrivance?* Why should not we be as *wise to do good*, as any people are *wise to do evil?* I am sure, we have a *better cause;* and there is more of *reason* for it. My friend, thou art one that makes but a *little figure* in the world, and a *brother of low degree*, behold, a vast encouragement! A *little* man may do a great deal of *hurt.* And then, why may not a *little* man, do a great deal of *good!* It is possible the *wisdom of a poor man*, may start a proposal, that may *save a city*, serve a nation! A *single hair* applied unto a *flyer*, that has other wheels depending on it, may pull up an *oak*, or pull down an *house*.

It is very observable, that when our Lord JESUS CHRIST would recommend the *zeal*, with which the *Kingdom of Heaven* is to be served, He did not mention an example of *honest wisdom;* no, but of an unrighteous and scandalous *dishonesty* (as of an *unjust steward*) [6] for our emulation. The *wisdom* of our Lord in this matter, is much to be observed. His design is, not only to represent the *prudence*, but also the vast industry, ingenuity, resolution, and *heroic effort of soul*, necessary in them, that would seek and serve the Kingdom of Heaven. There is nowhere to be found among men, that *vivacity of spirit* in *lawful* actions, which there is to be found in *unlawful* ones. The ways of *honesty* are plain to men, and they require not so much *uneasiness* in the minds of men to manage them. Whereas your *thieves* and *cheats*, and men that follow courses of *dishonesty*, take ways that are full of difficulties: the *turns* and the *tricks* with which they must be carried through them, are innumerable. Hence among such fellows, you find the exercise of the most extraordinary *subtlety*. There is no such cunning, and nimble *application* to be anywhere else met withal. 'Tis very emphatical, to fetch from hence the colors of *heavenly wisdom!* That which I would now be at, is this: that we *do good* with as much *application,* as any men alive can use in *evil-doing.* When *wickedness proceeds from the wicked,* it is often done *with both hands,* and *greedily.* Why may not we proceed in our *usefulness,* even *with both hands,* and *greedily* watching for opportunities? We have no occasion for any *ill arts,* that we may carry on our designs to *do good.* God forbid, that we should ever imagine the uniting of such *inconsistencies.* But why cannot we carry on our *designs,* with as much, and as deep, and as copious *thought,* as the men of *ill arts?* And why may not we lay out our spirits, with as transporting a vigor, to do the things that will be *acceptable* to God, and *profitable* to men, as any wretches have, when they *weary themselves to commit iniquity?* To reprehend certain ecclesiastical drones, who had little inclination to *do good,* Father *Latimer* [7] employed a coarse expression of this importance: "If you won't learn of good men, for shame learn of the Devil! He is never idle. He goes about, seeking what hurt he may do!" Truly, the indefatigable prosecution of their designs, which we may see in some, whom the Holy Word of God has called, *the children of the Devil,* may exceedingly put us to the blush. Our *obligations* to *do good* are infinite: they *do evil* against all *obligations.* The *compensations* made unto them who *do good,* are encouraging beyond all expression; they who *do evil,* get nothing to boast of; but *evil pursues the sinners.* If the *Devil* do *go about,* and people inspired by him also *go about, seeking what hurt they may do,* why do not we *go about,* and *seek,* and think, where and how to *do good?* Verily, 'twere a character for a *good angel,* to do so. O thou *child of God,* and *lover of all righteousness:* how canst thou find in thy heart at any time to *cease* from doing all the *good,* that can be done, in the *right ways of the Lord?*

Methinks, that *Word of the Lord,* may be a *burden* unto us; if we have any true *honor* in us, it will be so! *The children of this world, are in* (and *for*) *their generation, wiser than the children of light.* Yea, they pursue the *works of darkness* more livelily, than any of us *walk in the light,* wherewith our Great Saviour has favored us.

§7. To the title of GOOD WORKS there do belong, those *essays to do good,* which are now urged for. To produce them, the *first* thing, and indeed the ONE thing, that is *needful,* is, a glorious work of GRACE on the soul, renewing and quickening of it, and *purifying* of the sinner, and rendering him *zealous of good works:* a *workmanship of God* upon us, *creating* us over again, by JESUS CHRIST, *for good works.* And then, there is needful, what will necessarily follow upon such a *work:* that is, a *disposition* to *do good works* upon true, genuine, generous, and evangelical *principles.* Those *principles* are to be *stated,* before we can go any further; when they are *active,* we shall go a great deal further.

It is in the first place, to be taken for granted: that the *end* for which we do *good works* must not be, to afford the matter of our *justification,* before the Law of the holy GOD. Indeed, no *good works* can be done by any man until he be *justified.* Until a man be united unto the glorious CHRIST, who is *our life,* he is a *dead man.* And, I pray, what *good works* to be expected from such a man? They will all be *dead works.* For, "Severed from me ye can do nothing," saith our Saviour. The *justification of a* sinner, *by faith, before good works, and in order to them,* is one of those truths, which may say to the Popish innovations, "With us are the gray-headed, and very aged men, much elder than thy Father." It was an old maxim of the faithful, *Bona opera sequuntur justificatum, non præcedunt justificandum.*† It is the *righteousness* of the *good works* done by our Saviour and *Surety,* not our own, that

† Good works follow justification; they do not precede justification.

27

justifies us before God, and answers the demands of His Law upon us. We do by *faith* lay hold on those *good works* for our *justifying righteousness* before we arrive to do our own. 'Tis not our *faith* itself, either as doing of *good works*, or as being itself one of them, which entitles us to the *justifying righteousness* of our Saviour. But it is *faith*, only *as* renouncing of our own righteousness, and relying on that of our Saviour, provided for the *chief of sinners*, by which we are *justified*. Sir, all your attempts at *good works* will come to nothing, till a *justifying faith* in your Saviour, shall carry you forth unto them. This was the divinity of the ancients; *Jerome* has well expressed it: *Sine Christo omnis virtus est in vitie.*‡ Nevertheless; first, you are to look upon it, as a glorious truth of the Gospel, that the *moral law* (which prescribes and requires *good works*) must by every Christian alive be made the *rule* of his life. *Do we make void the Law through faith? God forbid. Yea, we establish the Law.* The *rule*, by which we are to *glorify* God, is given us in the law of *good works*, which we *enjoy* (I will express it *so!*) in the *Ten Commandments*. It is impossible for us, to be released from all obligations to glorify God by a conformity to this *rule;* sooner shall we cease to be creatures. The *conformity* to that rule in the *righteousness*, which our Saviour by His obedience to it, has *brought in*, to *justify* us, has forever *magnified the Law, and made it honorable*. Though our Saviour has furnished us, with a perfect and spotless *righteousness*, when His obedience to the *Law*, is placed unto our account; yet it is a *sin* for us at all to fall short in our own obedience to the *Law:* we must always loathe and judge ourselves for the *sin*. We are not under the *Law* as a *covenant of works*. Our own exactness in doing of *good works*, is not now the *condition* of our *entering into life. Woe unto us if it were!* But still, the *Covenant of Grace* holds us to it, as our *duty;* and if we are in the *Covenant of Grace*, we

‡ Without Christ, all virtue is vice.

shall make it our *study*, to *do* those *good works* which once
were the terms of our *entering into life*. *Manet lex tota pietatis;* § that was the divinity in *Tertullian's* [8] days! There must
be such an esteem for the *law* of *good works* retained forever
in all the *justified:* a *law* never to be abrogated; never to be
abolished! And then, secondly, though we are *justified* by a
precious faith in the *righteousness of God our Saviour*, yet
good works are demanded of us, to *justify* our *faith;* to *demonstrate*, that it is indeed that *precious faith*. A *justifying faith*
is a *jewel*, which may be *counterfeited*. But now the *marks* of a
faith, which is no counterfeit, are to be found in the *good
works* whereto a servant of God is inclined and assisted by his
faith. It is by a *regenerating work* of the Holy Spirit, that
faith is wrought in the souls of the chosen people. Now the
same *work* of God, and of *grace*, which does in a *regeneration*
dispose a man to make his flight by *faith*, unto the *righteousness*
of his only Saviour, will also dispose him to the *good works* of
a *Christian life*. And the same *faith* which goes to the Saviour
for a part in His *righteousness*, will also go to Him, for an heart
and strength to do the *good works*, which are *ordained, that we
should walk in them*. If our *faith* be not such a *faith*, 'tis a
lifeless one, and it will not bring to *life*. A *workless faith* is a
worthless faith. My friend, suppose thyself standing before the
Judgment-seat of the glorious LORD. A needful, a prudent, supposal; it ought to be a very *frequent* one. The *Judge* demands,
"What hast thou to plead, for a portion in the blessedness of the
righteous?" The plea must be:

"O my glorious Judge, Thou hast been my sacrifice. Oh!
Judge of all the earth, give poor dust and ashes leave to say, 'My
righteousness is on the bench. Surely in the Lord I have my
righteousness. O my Saviour, I have received it, I have secured
it, upon Thy gracious offer of it.' "

The *Judge* proceeds:

§ The entire law of duty [or obedience to God] remains.

"But what hast thou to plead, that thy faith should not be rejected, as the faith and hope of the hyprocrite?"

Here the plea must be:

"Lord, my faith was Thy work. It was a faith which disposed me to all the good works of Thy holy religion. My faith sanctified me. It carried me to Thee, O my Saviour, for grace to do the works of righteousness. It embraced that for my Lord as well as for my Saviour. It caused me with sincerity to love and keep Thy commandments; with assiduity to serve the interests of Thy Kingdom in the world." Thus you have *Paul* and *James* reconciled. Thus you have *good works* provided for. The aphorism of the physician, is, *Per brachium fit judicium de corde*. The *doings* of men are truer and surer indications, than all their *sayings*, of what they are *within*. But there is yet a further consideration, upon which you must be *zealously affected* for them. You must consider *good works*, as the *way* to, yea, as a *part* of, the *great salvation*, which is purchased and intended for you, by your blessed Saviour. Without an *holy heart* you can't be fit for an *holy heaven; meet for the inheritance of the holy ones* in that *light*, which admits no *works of darkness*, where none but *good works* are done for eternal ages. But an *holy heart* will cause a man to do *good works* with all his heart. The motto on the gates of the Holy City is: NONE BUT THE LOVERS OF GOOD WORKS TO ENTER HERE. 'Tis implied, in what we read, *without holiness no man shall see the Lord*. Yea, to be *saved* without *good works*, were to be *saved* without *salvation*. Much of our *salvation* lies in doing of *good works*. When our *souls* are *enlarged* and *unfettered*, it is that we may *do* such things. *Heaven* is begun upon *earth* in the doing of them. Doubtless, no man shall come up to *Heaven*, who is not so persuaded. I will mention but one more of those *principles*, which *good works* grow upon. 'Tis that noble one, of GRATITUDE. The believer cannot but inquire, "What shall I render to my Saviour?" The result of the inquiry will be, *with good works to glorify Him.* We read, "Faith works by love." Our *faith* will first show us the matchless and marvelous *love* of God, in saving us. And the *faith* of this *love* will work upon our hearts, until it has raised in us, an unquenchable flame of *love* unto Him that hath so *loved* us, and *saved* us.

These, these are to be our dispositions:

"O my Saviour, hast Thou done so much for me? Now will I do all I can for Thy Kingdom, and people in the world? Oh! What service is there that I may now do for my Saviour, and for His people in the world!"

These are the principles to be proceeded on! And on them, I will observe to you a notable thing. 'Tis worthy of observation, that there are no men in the world, who so abound in *good works,* as the men who have most of all abandoned all pretense to *merit* by their *works.* There are *Protestants* who have out-done *Papists,* in our days, as well as in Dr. *Willet's.*[9] No *merit-mongers* have gone beyond some holy Christians, who have done *good works,* upon the *assurance* of their being already justified and entitled unto life eternal.

I take notice, that our Apostle, casting a just contempt on the *endless genealogies,* and long, intricate, perplexed pedigrees, which the *Jews* of his time, stood so much upon; proposes instead thereof to be studied, *charity, out of a pure heart, and a good conscience, and faith unfeigned.*[10] As if he had said, I will give you a *genealogy* worth ten thousand of theirs, first, from *faith unfeigned* proceeds a *good conscience:* from a *good conscience* proceeds a *pure heart:* from a *pure heart* proceeds a *charity* to all about us. 'Tis admirably stated!

§8. It is to be feared, that we too seldom *inquire* after our Opportunities to Do Good. Our *opportunities to do good* are our Talents. An awful account must be rendered unto the great GOD, concerning our use of the Talents, wherewith He has entrusted us, in these precious *opportunities.* We do not *use* our *opportunities,* many times because we do not *know* what they are; and many times, the reason why we do not *know*, is because we do not *think*. Our *opportunities to do good*, lie by unregarded, and unimproved, and so 'tis but a mean account that can be given of them. We *read* of a thing, which we *deride* as often as we behold: *there is, that maketh himself poor, and yet has great riches.* It is a thing too freqently exemplified, in our *opportunities to do good*, which are some of our most valuable *riches.* Many a man seems to reckon himself destitute of those *talents;* as if there were *nothing* for him to do: he pretends he is not in a condition to *do* any *good. Alas! poor man; what can he do?* My friend, *think* again; *think* often. *Inquire* what your *opportunities* are. You will doubtless find them, to be more than you were *aware* of. *Plain men dwelling in tents*, persons of a very *ordinary character*, may in a way of bright piety, prove persons of *extraordinary usefulness.* A poor *John Urich* may make a *Grotius* the better for him.[11] I have read of a pious *Weaver*, of whom some eminent persons would say, "Christ walked as it were alive upon the Earth in that man." And a world of *good* was done by that man. A mean *mechanic*, who can tell what an *engine* of *good* he may be, if humbly and wisely applied unto it!

This then is the next PROPOSAL. Without abridging yourselves of your *occasional thoughts* on the question, often every day, *What good may I do?*, state a *time* now and then for more *deliberate thoughts* upon it. Can't you find a *time* (suppose once a week, yea, and how agreeably, on the *Lord's* day) to take that question into your consideration: WHAT IS THERE THAT I MAY DO, FOR THE SERVICE OF THE GLORIOUS LORD, AND FOR THE WELFARE OF THOSE, FOR WHOM I OUGHT TO BE CONCERNED? Having implored the *direction* of God, who is the *Father of Lights*, and the Author and Giver of *good thoughts, consider* on the matter, in the various aspects of it. *Consider* till you have *resolved* on something. The *resolutions* which you *take up*, immediately *write down.* Examine what *precept* and what *promise*, you can find in the Word of God, that may countenance the intentions, in these your *memorials*. Look over the *memorials* at proper seasons afterwards, to see how far you have proceeded in the execution of them. The advantages of these *reserved* and *revised* MEMORIALS, no *rhetoric* will serve to commend them, no *arithmetic* to number them. There are some *animals*, of whom we say, "They do not know their own strength." *Christians*, why should you be *they?*

§9. Let us descend unto PARTICULARS. But in doing so, let it not be imagined, that I pretend unto an enumeration of all the GOOD DEVICES, that are to be thought upon. Indeed, not a *thousandth* part of them, need or can be now enumerated. The *essay*, which I am now upon, is, only to dig open the several *springs* of *usefulness;* which having once begun to run, will spread into *streams*, which no *human foresight* can comprehend. *Spring up, O well!* [12] So will every true *Israelite* sing, upon every PROPOSAL here exhibited. And the *nobles of Israel* can do nothing more agreeable to their own character, than to fall to work upon it. Perhaps almost every *proposal* to be now mentioned, may be like a *stone* falling on a *pool; reader*, keep thy mind *calm*, and see, whether the effect prove not so! That one *circle* (and *service*) will produce another, until they extend, who can tell, how far? and they cannot be reckoned up. The men who give themselves up to GOOD DEVICES, and who take a due notice of their *opportunities to do good*, usually find a strange growth of their *opportunities*. The gracious and faithful Providence of the glorious Lord, grants this recompense unto His diligent servants, that He will *multiply* their *opportunities* to be *serviceable*. And when ingenious men have a little used themselves unto *contrivances*, in this or that way of pursuing the best intentions, their ingenuity will sensibly improve, and there will be more of *exquisiteness*, more of *expansion*, in their diffusive applications. Among all the dispensations of *special Providence*, in the government of the world, there is none more *uninterrupted*, than the accomplishment of that word, Unto Him That Hath, Shall Be Given. I will say this: O *useful Man*, take that for thy *motto:* Habenti Dabitur. And, in a lively use of thy *opportunities to do good*, see how notably, it will be accomplished! Sir, see what accomplishment of that word will at last surprise you: "Though thy beginning were small, yet thy latter end shall greatly increase." [13]

[CHAPTER TWO: THE DUTY TO ONESELF]

§ 10. *Odi sapientem qui sibi non sapit.*|| The *charity* we are upon, why should it not *begin at home?* It observes not a due *decorum,* if it do not so; and it will be liable to great exceptions in its pretensions and proceedings.

This then is to be made as an early PROPOSAL.

First, let every man *devise* what *good* may be done, for the help of what is yet amiss, IN HIS OWN HEART AND LIFE. It is a good note of the witty *Fuller's:* "He need not complain of too little work, who hath a little world in himself to mend." [1] It was of old complained: "No man repented him, saying, 'What have I done?' " [2] Every man upon earth may find in himself something that wants mending; and the work of *repentance* is to inquire, not only, *what we have done,* but also, *what we have to do?* Frequent SELF-EXAMINATION, is the duty and the prudence, of all that would *know themselves,* or would not *lose themselves.* The great intention of SELF-EXAMINATION is, to find out, the points, wherein we are to *amend our ways.* A Christian that would thrive in Christianity, must be no stranger to a course of MEDITATION. *Meditation,* 'tis one of the *masters* to make a *man of God.* One article and exercise in our *meditation,* should be, to find out, the things wherein a greater *conformity* to the *truths* upon which we have been meditating, must be endeavored. If we would be *good men,* we must often *devise,* how we may grow in *knowledge, and in all goodness!* It is an inquiry often to be made:

"What shall I do, that what is yet lacking in the image of God upon me, may be perfected? What shall I do, that I may live more perfectly, more watchfully, more fruitfully before the glorious Lord?"

|| I hate the wise man who does not know himself.

35

And why should not our *meditation*, when we retire to that *soul-enriching* work of shaping the *right thoughts of the right-eous*, expire with some *resolution! Devise* now, and *resolve* something, to strengthen your *walk with God*.

With some devout *hearers* of the Word, it is a practice, when they have heard a sermon, to think: "What good thing have I now to ask of God, with a special importunity?" Yea, they use to call upon their *children* also, and make them answer this question: "Child, what blessing will you now ask of the glorious God?" And charge them then to go, and do accordingly.

In pursuance of this piety, why may not this be one of the exercises, that shall go to make with us a *good evening for the best of days?* On the *Lord's-Day evening*, we may make this one of our exercises: to employ most serious and awful thoughts on that question: "Should I die this week, what have I left undone, which I should then wish I had made more speed in the doing of?" My friend, place thyself in *dying* circumstances; apprehend and realize thy approaching *death*. Suppose thy last hour come; the *decretory hour:* thy breath failing, thy throat rattling, thy hands with a cold sweat upon them, only the turn of the tide expected for thy expiration. In this condition, *what wouldst thou wish to have done, more than thou hast already done, for thy own soul, for thy family, or for the people of God?* Think; don't *forget* the result of thy thoughts; don't *delay* to do what thou hast resolved upon. How much more agreeable and profitable, would such an exercise be on the *Lord's-Day evening*, than those vanities whereto that *evening* is too commonly prostituted, and all the *good* of the foregoing *day* defeated? And if such an exercise were often attended, Oh! how much would we regulate our lives; how watchfully, how fruitfully would it cause us to live; what an incredible number of *good works* would it produce in the world?

Will you remember, Sirs, every Christian is *a temple of God*. It would be a service to Christianity, if this notion of Christianity were more often, and clearly cultivated. But certainly, there yet remains very much, for every one of us to do, that so the *temple* may be carried on unto perfection; repaired, finished, purified; and the top-stone of it laid, with a shout of *Grace! Grace!* unto it.

As a branch of this piety, I will recommend a serious and fruitful improvement, of the various *dispensations*, which the Divine Providence obliges us, to take notice of.

More particularly:

Have you received any *special blessings* and *mercies*, from the hand of a merciful God? You do not suitably express your thankfulness. You do not *render again according to the benefit that is done unto you;* except you set yourself to consider, *What shall I render to the Lord?* You should contrive some *signal thing* to be done on this occasion; some *service* to the Kingdom of God, either within yourself, or among others, that may be a just confession and remembrance of what a good God has done for you. 'Tis what the *goodness of God leads* you to! I beseech you, Sirs; how can a *good voyage,* yea, or a *good bargain* be made, without some *special returns* of *gratitude* unto God? I would now have something of your *estates* made a *thank-offering,* in being set apart for *pious uses.*

Whole *days of thanksgiving* are to be kept, when the favors of God rise to a more observable height. Christians of the finer mold keep their *private* ones, their *secret* ones, as well as bear their part in the *public.* One exercise for such a day is, to take a *list* of the more distinguishable succors, and bounties, where-with our God has comforted us. And then, to contrive some *notable acknowledgments* of the glorious Lord, in endeavors to serve Him, and this by way of *gratitude* for these undeserved comforts.

On the other hand. You meet with heavy and grievous *afflictions.* Verily, 'tis pity to be at the trouble of suffering *afflictions,* and not *get good* by them. We *get good* by them, when they awaken us to *do good*. I may say, never till then! When God is *distributing sorrows* unto you, the *sorrows* come still upon some *errands:* The best way for you to find, that they do not come *in His anger*, is for you to mind the *errands*. The advice is, that when any *affliction* comes upon you, you immediately consider, "What special article of repentance does this affliction call me to? What miscarriage does this affliction find in me, to be repented of?" And then, while the sense of the *affliction* is yet upon you, solicitously consider, "What improvement in godliness and usefulness does this affliction call me to?" Be more solicitous to gain this point, than to get out of your *affliction*. Oh! the *peace* that will compose and possess and ravish your minds, when your *affliction* shall be found yielding the *fruits of righteousness!*

Luther did well to call afflictions, *theologiam Christianorum.*¶ This may be a fit place, to introduce one direction more. We are travelling through a *malicious* and *calumnious*, and *abusive* world. Why should not *malice* be a *good informer?* We may be unjustly *defamed;* it will be strange if we are not frequently so. A *defamation* is commonly resented as a *provocation*. My friend, make it only a *provocation to good works!* The thing to be now directed is this. Upon any *reproach*, instead of being transported into a rage at *Shimei*,³ retire, and patiently ponder, "Has not God bidden such a reproach, to awaken me unto some duty? Unto what special instance or service of piety, should I be awakened, by the reproach that is cast upon me!" One thus expresses it: "The backbiter's tongue, like a mill-clack will be still wagging, that he may grind thy good name to powder. Learn therefore to make such use of his clack as to make thy bread by it; I mean, to live so, that no credit shall be given to slander." Thus all the *abuses* you meet withal, may prove unto you in the hand of a faithful God, no other than the strokes which a statuary employs on his ill-shaped marble; only to form

¶ the theology of Christians.

you into a more beautiful shape, and make you fitter to adorn the heavenly temple. Sirs, you are put into, a way to *shake off a viper,* how advantageously!

Yea, I am going to show you, how you may *fetch a treacle out of a viper.*[4] *Austin* would have our very *sins,* come into the invoice of the, *all things,* that are to *work together for good.* Wherefore, first, I move, that our former *barrenness* may now be looked upon, as our obligation and incitation to a greater *fruitfulness.* But this motion is too general. I will descend unto a notable particularity. I would look back, upon my past life, and call to mind what more *singular out-breakings of sin* have blemished it, and been the *reproach of my youth.* Now, by way of *thankfulness* for that *grace* of God, and that *blood* of His *Christ,* through which my *crimes* have been pardoned, I would set myself to think, "What virtues, and what actions, and what achievements for the Kingdom of God, will be the most contrary to my former blemishes? And what efforts of goodness, will be the noblest and most palpable contradiction to the miscarriages, with which I have been chargeable?" Yet more particularly, "What signal thing shall I do, to save others from dishonoring the great God by such miscarriages, as I myself once fell into?" I will study such things. Perhaps, the sincerity and consolation of *repentance,* cannot be better studied, than by such a conduct.

You shall give me leave, to press this one more *point of prudence* upon you. There are not a few persons, who have many *hours of leisure* in the way of their *personal callings.* When the *weather* takes them off their business, or when their *shops* are not full of customers, they have *little* or *nothing* to do; now, Sirs, the PROPOSAL is, *Be not fools,* but *redeem* this *time* to your own advantage, to the best advantage. To the *man of leisure,* as well as to the *minister,* it is an advice of wisdom, *Give thyself unto reading.* Good BOOKS of all sorts, may employ your *leisure,* and enrich you with treasures more valuable, than those, which the way and work of your callings would have purchased. Let the baneful *thoughts of idleness* be chased out of our minds. But then also, let some thoughts on that subject, *What good may I do?* come into them. When you have *leisure* to think on that subject, you can have no *excuse* for not thinking on it.

[CHAPTER THREE: RELATIVE TO HOME AND NEIGHBORHOOD]

§11. The *useful man* may now with a very good grace, extend and enlarge the *sphere* of his consideration. My next PROPOSAL now shall be: Let every man consider the RELATION, wherein the Sovereign God has placed him, and let him *devise what good he may do*, that may render his *relatives*, the better for him. One great way to prove ourselves *really good*, is to be *relatively good*. By this, more than by anything in the world, it is, that we *adorn the doctrine of God our Saviour*. It would be an *excellent wisdom* in a man, to make the *interest* he has in the good opinion and affection of *anyone*, an *advantage* to do good service for God upon them: He that *has a friend* will show himself indeed *friendly*, if he thinks, "Such an one loves me, and will hearken to me; what good shall I take advantage hence to persuade him to?"

This will take place more particularly, where the endearing ties of *natural relation* do give us an *interest*. Let us call over our several *relations*, and let us have *devices* of something that may be called *heroical goodness*, in our discharging of them. Why should we not, at least once or twice in a *week*, make this *relational goodness*, the subject of our *inquiries*, and our *purposes?* Particularly, let us begin with our *domestic relations*, and *provide for those of our own house*, lest we *deny* some glorious rules and hopes of our Christian *faith*, in our negligence.

First, in the CONJUGAL RELATION, how agreeably may the *consorts* think on those words: "What knowest thou, O wife, whether thou shalt save thy husband?" Or, "How knowest thou, O man, whether thou shalt save thy wife?"

The HUSBAND will do well to think: "What shall I do, that

my wife may have cause forever to bless God, for bringing her unto me?" And, "What shall I do that in my carriage towards my wife, the kindness of the blessed Jesus towards His Church, may be followed and resembled?" That this question may be the more perfectly answered, Sir, sometimes ask her to help you in the answer; ask her to tell you, what she would have you to do.

But then, the WIFE also will do well to think: "Wherein may I be to my husband, a wife of that character: she will do him good, and not evil, all the days of his life?"

With my *married people*, I will particularly leave a good note, which I find in the Memorials of *Gervase Disney*, Esq.[1] "Family passions, cloud faith, disturb duty, darken comfort." You'll do the more good unto one another, the more this note is thought upon. When the *husband* and *wife* are always contriving to be *blessings* unto one another, I will say with *Tertullian, Unde sufficiam ad enarrandam faelicitatem ejus matrimonii!* * O happy marriage!

PARENTS, Oh! how much ought you to be continually *devising*, and even *travailing*, for the *good* of your *children*. Often *devise:* how to make them *wise children;* how to carry on a desirable *education* for them; an *education* that shall render them desirable; how to render them lovely, and polite creatures, and *serviceable* in their generation. Often *devise*, how to enrich their minds with valuable *knowledge;* how to instill generous, and gracious, and heavenly *principles* into their minds; how to restrain and rescue them from the *paths of the Destroyer*, and fortify them against their *special temptations*. There is a world of *good*, that you have to do for them. You are without *bowels*, Oh! be not such *monsters!* if you are not in a continual agony to do for them all the *good* that ever you can. It was no mistake of *Pacatus Drepanius* [2] in his panegyric to *Theodosius: Instituente natura plus fere filios quam nosmetipsos diligimus.*†

* How can I find words to express the happiness of their marriage!
† Nature teaches us to love our children as ourselves.

42

I will prosecute this matter, by transcribing a copy of PAR-
ENTAL RESOLUTIONS, which I have somewhere met withal.[3]

I. "At the birth of my children, I would use all *explicit solemnity* in the *baptismal* dedication and consecration of them
unto the LORD. I would present them to the BAPTISM of the
Lord, not as a mere formality; but wondering at the grace of
the infinite GOD, who will accept *my* children, as *His*, I would
resolve to do all I can that they may be *His*. I would now actually give them up unto GOD; entreating, that the child may
be a *child* of God the *Father*, a *subject* of God the *Son*, a temple
of God the *Spirit*, and be rescued from the condition of a *child
of wrath*, and be possessed and employed by the Lord as an
everlasting instrument of His glory.

II. "My children are no sooner grown capable of minding the
admonitions, but I would often, often admonish them to be
sensible of their *baptismal engagements* to be the Lord's. Often
tell them, of their *baptism*, and of what it binds 'em to: oftener
far, and more times than there were *drops of water*, that were
cast on the infant, upon that occasion!

"Often say to them, 'Child, you have been baptized; you were
washed in the name of the great God; now you must not sin
against Him; to sin is to do a dirty, a filthy thing.' Say, 'Child,
you must every day cry to God that He would be your Father,
and your Saviour, and your Leader; in your baptism He promised that He would be so, if you sought unto Him.' Say, 'Child,
you must renounce the service of Satan, you must not follow the
vanities of this world, you must lead a life of serious religion;
in your baptism you were bound unto the service of your
only Saviour.' Tell the child: 'What is your name; you must
sooner forget this name, that was given you in your baptism,
than forget that you are a servant of a glorious Christ whose
name was put upon you in your baptism.'

III. "Let my *prayers* for my *children* be daily, with con-
stancy, with fervency, with agony; yea, *by name* let me mention each one of them, every day before the Lord.[4] I would

importunately beg for all suitable blessings to be bestowed upon them: that God would *give them grace, and give them glory, and withhold no good thing from them;* that God would *smile on their education, and give His good angels the charge over them, and keep them from evil, that it may not grieve them;* that when *their father and mother shall forsake them, the Lord may take them up.* With importunity I would plead that promise on their behalf: *the Heavenly Father will give the Holy Spirit unto them that ask Him.* Oh! happy children, if by *asking* I may obtain the *Holy Spirit* for them!

IV. "I would betimes entertain the children, with delightful *stories* out of the Bible. In the talk of the *table,* I would go through the *Bible,* when the *olive-plants about my table* are capable of being so *watered.* But I would always conclude the *stories* with some *lessons* of piety, to be inferred from them.

V. "I would single out some *Scriptural sentences,* of the greatest importance; and some also that have *special antidotes* in them against the common errors and vices of children. They shall quickly get those *golden sayings* by heart, and be rewarded with *silver* or *gold,* or some good thing, when they do it. Such as,

Psalm 111. 10.
The fear of the Lord, is the beginning of wisdom.
Matth. 16. 26
What is a man profited, if he gain the whole world,
and lose his own soul.
I. Tim. 1. 15.
JESUS CHRIST came into the world to save
sinners, of whom I am chief.
Matth. 6. 6.
Enter into thy closet, and when thou hast shut thy door,
pray to thy Father which is in secret.
Eccl. 12. 14.

God shall bring every work into judgment, with every
secret thing.

Eph. 5. 25.

Put away lying, speak everyone the truth.

Psalm 138. 6.

The Lord hath respect unto the lowly, but the proud
He knows afar off.

Rom. 12. 17, 19.

Recompense to no one evil for evil. Dearly beloved,
avenge not yourselves.

Neh. 13. 18.

They bring wrath upon Israel, by profaning the
Sabbath.

"A Jewish treatise quoted by *Wagenseil*,[5] tells us, that
among the Jews, when a child began to speak, the father was
bound to teach him that verse: Deut. 33. 4, 'Moses commanded
us a Law, even the inheritance of the Congregation of Jacob.'
Oh! let me betimes make my children acquainted with the
Law which our blessed JESUS has *commanded* us! 'Tis the
best *inheritance* I can derive unto them.

VI. "I would betimes cause my children to learn the *Catechism*. In *catechizing* of them, I would break the answer into
many lesser and proper *questions;* and by their answer to them,
observe and quicken their *understandings*. I would bring every
truth, into some *duty* and *practice*, and expect them to *confess*
it, and *consent* unto it, and *resolve* upon it. As we go on in our
catechizing, they shall, when they are able, turn to the *proofs*,
and *read* them, and say to me, *what* they prove, and *how*.
Then, I will take my times, to put nicer and harder *questions* to
them; and improve the times of conversation with my family
(which every man ordinarily has or may have) for conferences
on matters of religion.

VII. "Restless would I be, till I may be able to say of my

children, 'Behold, they pray!' I would therefore teach them to *pray.* But after they have learnt a *form of prayer,* I will press them, to proceed unto points which are not in their *form.* I will show them the *state of their own souls;* and on every stroke inquire of them, *what they think ought now to be their prayer.* I will direct them, that every morning they shall take one text or two out of the *Sacred Scripture,* and shape it into a *desire,* which they shall add unto their *usual prayer.* When they have heard a *sermon,* I will mention to them over again the main subject of it, and ask them thereupon, *what they have now to pray for.* I will charge them, with all possible cogency, to *pray in secret;* and often call upon them, 'Child, I hope, you don't forget my charge to you, about secret prayer: your crime is very great, if you do!'

VIII. "I would betimes do what I can, to beget a *temper of benignity* in my *children,* both towards one another, and towards all other people. I will instruct them how ready they should be to *communicate unto others,* a part of what they have; and they shall see, my encouragements, when they discover a *loving,* a *courteous,* an *helpful* disposition. I will give them now and then a piece of money, for them with their own little hands to dispense unto the poor. Yea, if any one has *hurt* them, or *vexed* them, I will not only forbid them all *revenge,* but also oblige them to do a *kindness* as soon as may be to the *vexatious* person. All *coarseness* of *language* or *carriage* in them, I will discountenance it.

IX. "I would be solicitous to have my *children* expert, not only at *reading* handsomely, but also at *writing* a fair hand. I will then assign them such *books* to *read,* as I may judge most agreeable and profitable; obliging them to give me some account of what they *read;* but keep a strict eye upon them, that they don't stumble on *the Devil's library,* and poison themselves with foolish *romances,* or *novels,* or *plays,* or *songs,* or *jests that are not convenient.* I will set them also, to *write* out such things, as may be of the greatest benefit unto them; and they shall have their blank books, neatly kept on purpose, to enter such passages as I advise them to. I will particularly require them now and then, to *write* a *prayer* of their own composing, and bring it unto me; that so I may discern, what sense they have of their own everlasting interests.

X. "I wish that my *children* may as soon as may be, feel the principles of *reason* and *honor*, working in them, and that I may carry on their education, very much upon those principles. Therefore, first, I will wholly avoid, that harsh, fierce, crabbed usage of the children, that would make them tremble, and abhor to come into my presence. I will so use them, that they shall *fear* to offend me, and yet mightily *love* to see me, and be glad of my coming home, if I have been abroad at any time. I would have it looked upon as a severe and awful *punishment* for a crime in the family, to be *forbidden for awhile to come into my presence*. I would raise in them, an high opinion of their father's *love* to them, and of his being *better able* to judge what is good for them, than they are for themselves. I would bring them to believe, *'tis best for them to be and do as I would have them*. Hereupon I would continually magnify the matter to them, what a brave thing 'tis to *know* the things that are excellent; and more brave to *do* the things that are virtuous. I would have them to propose it as a *reward* of their well-doing at any time, *I will now go to my father, and he will teach me something that I was never taught before*. I would have them afraid of doing any *base* thing, from an horror of the *baseness* in it. My first animadversion on a lesser fault in them, shall be a *surprise*, a *wonder*, vehemently expressed before them, that ever they should be guilty of doing so foolishly; a vehement *belief*, that they will never do the like again; a weeping resolution in them, that they will not. I will never dispense a *blow*, except it be for an atrocious crime, or for a lesser fault obstinately persisted in; either for an enormity, or for an *obstinacy*.

I would ever *proportion* chastisements unto miscarriages; not smite bitterly for a very small piece of *childishness*, and only frown a little for some real *wickedness*. Nor shall my *chatisements* ever be dispensed in a *passion* and a *fury;* but with them, I will first show them the command of GOD, by transgressing whereof they have displeased me. The slavish, raving, fighting way of education too commonly used, I look upon it, as a considerable article in the wrath and curse of God, upon a miserable world.

XI. "As soon as we can, we'll get up to yet *higher principles.* I will often tell the *children*, what cause they have to *love* a glorious CHRIST, who has *died* for them. And, how much He will be *well-pleased* with their *well-doing*. And, what a noble thing, 'tis to follow His *example;* which *example* I will describe unto them. I will often tell them, that the *eye of God* is upon them; the great GOD knows all they do, and hears all they speak. I will often tell them, that there will be a time, when they must appear before the *Judgment-Seat* of the holy LORD; and they must *now* do nothing, that may *then* be a grief and shame unto them. I will set before them, the delights of that *Heaven* that is prepared for pious children; and the torments of that *Hell* that is prepared of old, for naughty ones. I will inform them, of the *good offices* which the *good angels* do for *little ones* that have the fear of God, and are afraid of sin. And, how the *devils* tempt them to do ill things; how they hearken to the *devils*, and are like *them*, when they do such things; and what mischiefs the *devils* may get leave to do them in this world, and what a sad thing 'twill be, to be among the *devils* in the *Place of Dragons.* I will cry to God, that He *will make them feel the power of these principles.*

XII. "When the *children* are of a fit age for it, I will sometimes *closet* them; have them with me *alone;* talk with them about the state of their souls; their *experiences*, their *proficiencies*, their *temptations;* obtain their declared consent unto every stroke in the *Covenant of Grace;* and then pray with them, and weep unto the Lord for His *grace,* to be bestowed upon them, and make them witnesses of the agony with which I am *travailing* to see the image of CHRIST formed in them. Certainly, they'll never forget such actions!

XIII. "I would be very watchful and cautious, about the *companions* of my *children.* I will be very inquisitive, what *company* they keep; if they are in hazard of being ensnared by any *vicious company,* I will earnestly pull them out of it, as *brands out of the burning.* I will find out, and procure, *laudable companions* for them.

XIV. "As in *catechizing* the children, so in the *repetition* of the public sermons, I would use this method. I will put every *truth* into a *question,* to be answered still, with *Yes,* or *No.* By this method, I hope to awaken their *attention* as well as enlighten their *understanding.* And thus I shall have an opportunity to ask, 'Do you desire such or such a grace of God?' and the like. Yea, I may have opportunity to demand, and perhaps to *obtain* their early, and frequent, and why not *sincere?, consent* unto the glorious articles of the *New Covenant.* The *Spirit of Grace* may fall upon them in this action; and they may be seized by Him, and held as His *temples,* through eternal ages.

XV. "When a Day of *Humiliation* arrives, I will make them know the *meaning* of the Day. And after time given them to consider of it, I will order them to tell me: *what special afflictions they have met withal?* And, *what good they hope to get by those afflictions?* On a Day of *Thanksgiving,* they shall also be made to know the *intent* of the Day. And after consideration, they shall tell me, *what mercies of God unto them they take special notice of:* And, *what duties to God, they confess and resolve, under such obligations?* Indeed, for something of this importance, to be pursued in my conversation with the children, I would not confine myself unto the *solemn Days,* which may occur too seldom for it. Very particularly, when the *birthdays* of the children anniversarily arrive to any of them, I would then take them aside, and mind them of the *age*, which *having obtained help from God* they are come unto; how *thankful* they should be for the mercies of God, which they have hitherto lived upon; how *fruitful* they should be in all goodness, that so they may still enjoy their mercies. And I would inquire of them, whether they have ever yet begun to mind the *work* which God sent them into the world upon; how far they understand the work; and what good strokes they have struck at it; and, how they design to spend the rest of their time, if God still continue them in the world.

XVI. "When the *children* are in any *trouble*, as, if they be *sick*, or *pained*, I will take advantage therefrom, to set before them the evil of *sin*, which brings all our *trouble;* and how fearful a thing it will be to be cast among the *damned*, who are in easeless and endless *trouble*. I will set before them the benefit of an interest in a CHRIST, by which their *trouble* will be sanctified unto them, and they will be prepared for *death*, and for fullness of joy in an happy eternity after *death*.

XVII. "I incline, that among all the points of a polite education which I would endeavor for my *children*, they may each of them, the *daughters* as well as the *sons*, have so much insight into some *skill*, which lies in the way of *gain* (the *limners*', or the *scriveners*', or the *apothecaries*', or some other *mystery*, to which their own inclination may most carry them) that they may be able to subsist themselves, and get something of a livelihood, in case the Providence of God should bring them into necessities. Why not they as well as *Paul the Tent-Maker!* The *children* of the best fashion, may have occasion to bless the parents, that make such a provision for them! The Jews have a saying; 'tis worth my remembering it: *Quicunque filium suum non docet opificium, perinde est ac si eum doceret latrocinium.*‡

XVIII. "As soon as ever I can, I would make my children

‡ He who does not teach his son a craft, teaches him theft.

apprehensive of the main END, for which they are to *live;* that so they may as soon as may be, *begin to live;* and their *youth* not be nothing but *vanity.* I would show them, that their main END must be, *to acknowledge the great* GOD, *and His glorious* CHRIST; *and bring others to acknowledge Him:* and that they are never *wise* nor *well,* but when they are doing so. I would show them, what the *acknowledgments* are, and how they are to be made. I would make them able to answer the grand question, *why they live; and what is the end of the actions that fill their lives?* Teach them, how their *Creator* and *Redeemer* is to be obeyed in everything; and, how everything is to be done in *obedience* to Him; teach them, how even their *diversions,* and their *ornaments,* and the *tasks* of their education, must all be to fit them for the *further service* of Him, to whom I have devoted them; and how in these also, His commandments must be the rule of all they do. I would sometimes therefore surprise them with an inquiry, 'Child, what is this for? Give me a good account, why you do it?' How comfortably shall I see them *walking in the light,* if I may bring them *wisely* to answer this inquiry; and what *children of the light?*

XIX. "I would oblige the *children,* to retire sometimes, and ponder on that question: 'What shall I wish to have done, if I were now a-dying?' And report unto me, their *own answer* to the question; of which I would then take advantage, to inculcate the *lessons of godliness* upon them. I would also direct them and oblige them, at a proper time for it, seriously to realize, their own appearance before the awful *Judgment-Seat* of the Lord JESUS CHRIST, and consider, *what they have to plead, that they may not be sent away into everlasting punishment; what they have to plead, that they may be admitted into the Holy City.* I would instruct them, what *plea* to prepare; first, show them, how to get a part in the *righteousness* of Him that is to be their *Judge;* by receiving it with a thankful *faith,* as the *gift* of infinite grace unto the distressed and unworthy sinner: then, show them how to prove that their *faith* is not a counterfeit, by their continual endeavor to please Him in all things, who is to be their *Judge,* and to serve His Kingdom and interest in the world. And I would charge them, to make this preparation.

XX. "If I live to see the children *marriageable,* I would, before I consult with Heaven and earth for their best accommodation in the *married state,* endeavor the *espousal* of their souls unto their only *Saviour.* I would as plainly, and as fully as I can, propose unto them, the terms on which the glorious Redeemer would *espouse* them to Himself, *in righteousness and judgment, and favor, and mercies forever;* and solicit their consent unto His proposals and overtures. Then would I go on, to do what may be expected from a tender parent for them, in their *temporal circumstances.*"

From these *parental resolutions,* how *naturally,* how *reasonably* may we pass on to say:

"CHILDREN, the *Fifth Commandment* confirms all your other numberless and powerful obligations, often to *devise,* 'Wherein may I be a blessing to my parents?' *Ingenuity* would make this the very top of your *ambition;* to be a *credit,* and a *comfort* of your *parents;* to *sweeten,* and if it may be, to *lengthen* the *lives* of those, from whom, under God, you have received *your lives.* And *God the Rewarder* usually gives it, even *in this life,* a most observable recompense. But it is possible, you may be the happy instruments of more than a little *good* unto the *souls* of your *parents* (will you think, *how!*); yea, though they should be pious parents, you may by some exquisite methods, be the instruments of their growth in piety, and in preparation for the Heavenly world. *O thrice and four times happy children!* Among the Arabians, a father sometimes takes his name from an eminent SON, as well as a son from his reputed father. A man is called with an *Abu,* as well as an *Ebn.* Verily, a son may be such a blessing to his father that the best surname for the glad father would be, *the father of such an one.*"

MASTERS, yea, and MISTRESSES too, must have their *devices, how to do good unto their servants;* how to make them the *servants* of Christ, and the *children* of God. God whom you must remember to be *your Master in Heaven,* has brought them, and put them into your hands. Who can tell what *good* He has brought them for? How if they should be the *elect* of God, fetched from *Africa,* or the *Indies,* and brought into your families, on purpose, that by the means of their being *there,* they may be brought home unto the *Shepherd of Souls?* [6] Oh! that the *souls* of our *slaves,* were of more account with us! that we gave a better demonstration that we *despise not our own souls,* by doing what we can for the *souls* of our *slaves,* and not using them as if they had no *souls!* that the poor *slaves* and *blacks,* which live with us, may by our means be made the *candidates* of the Heavenly life! How can we pretend unto *Christianity,* when we do no more to *Christianize* our *slaves!* Verily, you must give an *account* unto God, concerning *them.* If they be lost, through your negligence, what answer can you make unto *God the Judge of all!* Methinks, common principles of gratitude should incline you, to study the happiness of those, by whose obsequious labors, your lives are so much accommodated. Certainly, they would be the *better servants* to you, the more faithful, the more honest, the more industrious, and submissive *servants* to you, for your bringing them into the service of your *common Lord.*

But if any servant of God, may be so honored by Him, as to be made the successful instrument, of obtaining from a *British* Parliament, *an act for the Christianizing of the slaves in the Plantations;* then it may be hoped, something more may be done, than has yet been done, that the *blood of souls* may not be found in the *skirts* of our nation: a *controversy* of Heaven with our Colonies may be removed, and *prosperity* may be restored; or, however [whoever?] the honorable instrument, will have unspeakable *peace* and *joy,* in the remembrance of his endeavors.

In the meantime, the *slave-trade* is a spectacle that shocks *humanity*.

> *The harmless natives basely they trepan,*
> *And barter baubles for the* souls of men.
> *The wretches they to Christian climes bring o'er*
> *To serve worse heathens than they did before.*

I have somewhere met with a paper under this title, "The Resolution of a Master," which may here afford an agreeable paragraph and parenthesis.[7]

I. "I would always remember, that my *servants* are in some sort my *children*. In a care, *that they may want nothing that may be good for them*, I would make them as my *children*. And, as far as the *methods of instilling piety*, which I use with my *children*, may be properly and prudently used with these, they shall be partakers in them. Nor will I leave them ignorant of anything, wherein I may *instruct* them to be useful in their generation.

II. "I will see that my *servants* be furnished with *Bibles*, and able and careful to *read* the *lively oracles*. I will put both *Bibles* and other good and fit books into their hands; and allow them *time* to *read*, but assure myself that they don't *misspend* this time. If I can discover any *wicked books* in their hands, I will take away from them, those pestilential *instruments of wickedness*. They shall also *write* as well as *read*, if I can bring them to it. And I will set them now and then such things to *write*, as may be for their greatest advantage.

III. "I will have my *servants* present at the religious exercises of my *family;* and let fall either in the *speeches,* or in the *prayers,* of the *daily sacrifice* in the family, such passages, as may have a tendency to quicken a sense of religion in them.

IV. "The *catechizing* stroke as far as the *age* or *state* of the *servants* will permit, that it may be done with decency, shall extend unto them also. And they shall be concerned in the *conferences,* wherein the repetition of the public sermons, may engage me with my *family.* If any of them, when they come to me, have not learnt the *Catechism,* I will see to it, that they shall do it, and give them a *reward* when they have done it.

V. "I will be very *inquisitive* and *solicitous* about the *company* chosen by my *servants;* and with all possible cogency rescue them from the snares of *evil company:* forbid their being the *companions of fools.*

VI. "Such of my *servants* as may be employed for that purpose, I will employ to teach *lessons of piety* unto my *children,* and recompense them for doing so. But I would with a particular *artifice* contrive them to be such *lessons,* as may be for their own edification too.

VII. "I will sometimes call my *servants* alone; talk with them about the *state of their souls;* tell them how to close with their only *Saviour;* charge them to do well, and *lay hold on eternal life;* and show them very particularly, how they may render all the *service* they do for *me,* a service to the glorious *Lord;* how they may do all from a principle of obedience to the Lord, and become entitled unto the *reward of the Heavenly inheritance.*" [8]

I make this appendix to these RESOLUTIONS. I have read such a passage as this:

"*Age* is well nigh sufficient with some *masters* to obliterate every letter and action, in the history of a meritorious life; and *old services* are generally buried under the ruins of an *old carcass.*" And this passage, "It's a barbarous inhumanity in men towards their servants, to make their small failings to be a crime, without allowing their past services to have been a virtue. *Good God, keep thy servant from such ingratitude!* Worse than *villainous* ingratitude!"

But then, O SERVANTS, if you would arrive to the *reward of the inheritance,* you should set yourselves to *devise:* "How shall I approve myself such a servant, that the Lord may bless the house of my master, the more for my being in it?" Certainly, there are many ways, wherein *servants* may be *blessings*. Let your *studies* with your continual *prayers* for the welfare of the *families* to which you belong, and the *example* of your sober carriage, render you such. If you will remember but *four words*, and endeavor all that is comprised in them, OBEDIENCE, HONESTY, INDUSTRY, and PIETY, you will be the *blessings* and the *Josephs* [9] of the families to which you belong. Let those four heads, be distinctly and frequently thought upon. And go cheerfully through all you have to do, upon this consideration: *that it is an obedience to Heaven, and from thence will have a recompense.* It was the observation even of a pagan, *that a master may receive a benefit from a servant.* And, *Quod fit affectu amici, desinit esse ministerium.*§ It is a *friendship* rather than a *service, young man,* if it be with the affection of a *friend,* that you do what you do for your *master.* Yea, even the *maid-servants* in the house, may do an unknown *service* to it, by instructing the *infants,* and instilling the *lessons of goodness* into them. So, by *Bilhah,* and *Zilpah,*[10] may children be *born again;* the *mistresses* may by the *travail* of their *maid-servants,* have *children,* brought into the Kingdom of God.

I will go on. *Humanity* teaches us, to take notice of all that are our *kindred. Nature* bespeaks, that which we call a *natural affection* to all that are *akin* to us. To be without it, is a very bad character; 'tis a brand on the worst of *men;* on such as forfeit the name of *men.* But now, *Christianity* is to improve it. Our *natural affection* is to be improved into a *religious intention.* Sir, take a catalogue of all your more DISTANT RELATIVES. Consider them one after another; and make every one of them, the subjects of your *good devices.* Think: "Wherein may I pursue the good of such a relative?" And, "By what means may I render such a relative the better for me?" It is possible, you

§ What is done with the affection of a friend is no longer the act of a mere servant.

may do something, that may give them cause to bless God, that ever you have been *related* unto them. Have they no *calamity*, under which you may give them some relief? Is there no *temptation* against which you may give them some caution? Is there no article of their *prosperity*, to which you may be subservient? At least; with your affectionate *prayers*, you may go over your *catalogue;* you may successively pray for every one of them all by name; and, if you can, why should you not also put agreeable *books of piety* into their hands, to be lasting *remembrancers* of their *duties* to God, and of your *desires* for them?

§12. Methinks, this excellent zeal should be carried into our *neighborhood*. *Neighbors*, you stand *related* unto one another; and you should be full of *devices*, that all the *neighbors* may have cause to be glad of your being in the *neighborhood*. We read, "The righteous is more excellent than his neighbor." But we shall scarce own him so, except he be *more excellent* AS *a neighbor*. He must *excel* in the duties of *good neighborhood*. Let that man be *better* than his *neighbor*, who labors to be a *better neighbor;* to do most *good* unto *his neighbor*.

And here, first, the *poor* people that lie *wounded*, must have *wine* and *oil* poured into their *wounds*. It was a charming stroke in the character with [which?] a modern prince had given to him, *To be in distress, is to deserve his favor*. O good neighbor, put on that princely, that more than royal quality. See who in the neighborhood may *deserve thy favor*. We are told, *This is pure religion and undefiled* (a jewel, that neither is a counterfeit, nor has any flaws in it): *to visit the fatherless and widows in their affliction*.[11] The *orphans* and the *widows*, and so all the children of *affliction* in the neighborhood, must be *visited*, and relieved with all agreeable kindnesses.

Neighbors, be concerned, that the *orphans* and *widows* in your neighborhood, may be well provided for. *They* meet with grievous difficulties; with unknown temptations. While their next *relatives* were yet living, they were, perhaps, but meanly provided for. What must they now be in their more solitary condition? Their condition should be considered: and the result of the consideration should be that: *I delivered the orphan, that had no helper, and I caused the heart of the widow to sing for joy.*

By consequence, all the afflicted in the neighborhood, are to be thought upon. Sirs, would it be too much for you, at least *once in a week,* to think, "What neighbor is reduced into a pinching and painful poverty? Or in any degree impoverished with heavy losses?" Think, "What neighbor is languishing with sickness; especially if sick with sore maladies, and of some continuance?" Think, "What neighbor is heartbroken with sad bereavements; bereaved of desirable relatives?" And think: "What neighbor has a soul buffeted, and buried with violent assaults of the Wicked one?" But then think, "What shall be done for such neighbors?"

First, you will *pity* them. The evangelical precept is, *Have compassion one of another, be pitiful.* It was of old, and ever will be, the just expectation, *To him that is afflicted, pity should be shown.* And let our *pity* to them, flame out in our *prayer* for them. It were a very lovely practice for you, in the *daily prayer* of your *closet* every evening, to think, "What miserable object have I seen today, that I may do well now to mention for the mercies of the Lord?"

But this is not all. 'Tis possible, 'tis probable, you may do well to *visit* them; and when you *visit* them, *comfort* them. Carry them some *good word,* which may raise a *gladness,* in an *heart stooping with heaviness.*

And lastly. Give them all the *assistances* that may answer their *occasions:* assist them with *advice* to them; assist them with *address* to others for them. And if it be needful, bestow your ALMS upon them; *deal thy bread to the hungry; bring to thy house the poor that are cast out; when thou seest the naked, cover him*. At least, *Nazianzen's* charity, I pray: *Si nihil habes, da lacrymulam;* if you have nothing else to bestow upon the miserable, bestow a *tear* or two upon their miseries. This *little,* is better than *nothing!*

Would it be amiss for you, to have always lying by you, a list of the *poor* in your neighborhood, or of those whose *calamities* may call for the *assistances* of the neighborhood? Such a *list* would often furnish you, with matter for an *useful conversation,* when you are talking with your friends, whom you may *provoke to love and good works.*

I will go on to say: Be glad of *opportunities* to *do good* in your *neighborhood:* yea, look out for them, lay hold on them, with a rapturous assiduity. *Be sorry* for all the *bad circumstances* of any neighbor, that bespeak your *doing of good* unto him. Yet, *be glad,* if any one tell you of them. Thank him who tells you, as having therein done you a very great civility. Let him know, that he could not by anything have more gratified you. Any *civility* that you can show, by *lending,* by *watching,* by —all the methods of *courtesy;* show it; and be glad you can show it. Show it, and give a *pleasant countenance* (*cum munere vultum*) in the showing of it. Let your *wisdom* cause your *face* always to *shine;* look, not with a *cloudy* but a serene and *shining face,* upon your neighbors; and shed the rays of your *courtesy* upon them, with such affability, that they may see they are welcome to all you can do for them. Yea, stay not until you are told of *opportunites* to *do good.* Inquire after them; let the inquiry be solicitous, be unwearied. The incomparable pleasure, is worth an inquiry.

There was a generous pagan, who counted a *day lost,* if he had obliged nobody in the day. *Amici, diem perdidi!*|| O *Christian,* let us try whether we can't attain to do something, for some neighbor or other, every day that comes over our head. Some do so; and with a better spirit, than ever *Titus Vespasian* [12]

|| Friends, I have lost the day!

was acted withal. Thrice in the Scriptures, we find the good angels *rejoicing:* 'tis always, *at the good of others.* To *rejoice* in the *good* of others, and most of all in doing of *good* unto them, 'tis *angelical goodness.*

In moving for the *devices* of *good neighborhood*, a principal motion which I have to make, is, that you consult the *spiritual* interests of your neighborhood, as well as the *temporal.* Be concerned, lest the *deceitfulness of sin* undo any of the neighbors. If there be any *idle persons* among them, I beseech you, cure them of their *idleness;* don't nourish 'em and harden 'em in that; but find *employment* for them. Find 'em *work;* set 'em to *work;* keep 'em to *work. Then,* as much of your other bounty to them, as you please.

If any *children* in the neighborhood, are under no education, don't allow 'em to continue so. Let care be taken, that they may be better educated; and be taught to read; and be taught their *Catechism;* and the truths and ways of their only Saviour.

Once more. If any in the neighborhood, are taking to *bad courses*, lovingly and faithfully admonish them. If any in the neighborhood are enemies to their own welfare, or their families; prudently dispense your admonitions unto them. If there are any *prayerless families*, never leave off entreating and exhorting of them, till you have persuaded them, to set up the *worship* of God. If there be any *service* of God, or of His people, to which any one may need to be excited, give him a tender excitation. Whatever *snare* you see any one in, be so kind, as to tell him of his danger to be *ensnared*, and save him from it. By putting of *good books* into the hands of your neighbors, and gaining of them a promise to *read the books*, who can tell, what good you may do unto them! It is possible, you may in this way, with ingenuity, and with efficacy, administer those *reproofs*, which you may owe unto such neighbors, as are to be *reproved* for their miscarriages. The *books* will balk nothing, that is to be said, on the subjects, that you would have the neighbors advised upon.

Finally. If there be any *base houses*, which threaten to debauch, and poison, and confound the neighborhood, let your charity to your neighbors, make you do all you can, for the suppression of them.

That my PROPOSAL *To Do Good in the Neighborhood, and as a Neighbor,* may be more fully formed and followed; I will conclude it, with minding you, that a world of *self-denial* is to be exercised in the execution of it. You must be armed against *selfishness,* all *selfish* and *squinting* intentions, in your generous resolutions. You shall see how my demands will grow upon you.

First. You must not think of making the *good* you do, a pouring of water into a pump, to draw out something for yourselves. This might be the meaning of our Saviour's direction: *Lend, hoping for nothing again.*[13] To *lend* a thing, properly is to *hope* that we shall *receive it again.* But this probably refers to the, Ερανισμος, or *collation,* usual among the ancients, whereof we find many monuments and mentions in antiquity. If any man by burnings, or shipwrecks or other disasters, had lost his estate, his friends did use to *lend* him considerable sums of money, to be repaid, not at a certain day, but when he should find himself able to repay it, without inconvenience. Now, they were so cunning, that they would rarely *lend* upon such disasters, unto any but such, as they had *hope,* would recover out of their present impoverishment, and not only repay them their money, but also Αντερανιζειν *requite* their kindness, if ever there should be need of it. The thing required by our Saviour, is, *Do good unto such as you are never like to be the better for.*

But then, there is yet an higher thing to be demanded, that is: *Do good* unto those neighbors who have *done hurt* unto you. So says our Saviour, *Love your enemies, bless them that curse you, do good to them that hate you, and pray for them which despitefully use you and persecute you.*[14] Yea, if an *injury* have been done you, improve it as a provocation to do a *benefit* unto him who did the *injury*. This is noble. 'Twill bring marvellous consolations! Another method might make you *even* with your froward neighbors; this, will set you *above* them all. 'Twere nobly done, if in the close of the day, when you are alone before the Lord, you make a *particular prayer*, for the pardon and prosperity, of any person, from whom you may have suffered any abuse in the day. And it would be nobly done, if at last calling over the *catalogue* of such as have been abusive to you, you may be able to say (the only intention that can justify your doing anything like to keeping a *catalogue* of them!), "There is not one of these, but I have done him, or watched to do him, a kindness!" Among the *Jews* themselves, there were the *Hasideans,* one of whose institutions it was, to make this daily prayer unto God, *Remitte et condona omnibus qui vexant nos.*¶ *Christians,* go beyond them. Yea, *Justin Martyr* [15] tells us, in the primitive times they did so; υπερ των εχθρων ευχομενος, *praying for their enemies.*

But I won't stop here. There is yet an higher thing to be demanded. That is: *Do good* unto those neighbors, who will *speak ill* of you, after you have done it. So says our Saviour: *Ye shall be the children of the Highest; He is kind unto the unthankful, and unto the evil.*[16] You will every day find, I can tell you, *monsters of ingratitude.* Yea, if you *distinguish* any person, with doing for him, something more than you have done for others, it will be well if that very person do not at some time or other, hurt you wonderfully. Oh! the *wisdom* of *Divine Providence,* in ordering this thing! Sirs, it is, that you may *do good* on a *divine principle; good,* merely for the sake of *good! Lord, increase our faith!*

And God forbid, that a *Christian faith,* should not come up to

¶ Forgive all those who injure us.

62

a *Jewish!* There is a memorable passage, in the *Jewish* records:
"There was a gentleman, of whose bounty many people every
day received reliefs and succors. One day he asked: 'Well, what
do our people say today?' They told him, 'Why, the people
partook of your kindnesses, and services, and then they blessed
you very fervently.' 'Did they so,' said he; 'then I shall have no
great reward for this day.' Another day he asked, 'Well, and
what say our people now?' They told him, 'Alas, good Sir, the
people enjoyed your kindnesses today, and when all was done,
they did nothing but rail at you.' 'Indeed!' said he; 'now for
this day I am sure that God will give me a good and great reward.'"

Though vile constructions, and harsh invectives, be never so
much the *present reward* of doing the best offices for the neighborhood, yet, my dear *Boniface;* be victorious over all discouragements: *Thy work shall be well rewarded, saith the Lord!* [17]

If your opportunities to *do good* reach no further, yet I will
offer you a consolation, which one has elegantly thus expressed:
"He that praises God only on a ten-stringed instrument, with
his authority extending but unto his family, and his example
but unto his neighborhood, may have as thankful an heart here,
and as high a place in the celestial choir hereafter, as the greatest
monarch, that praiseth God upon a ten-thousand-stringed instrument, upon the loud sounding organs, having as many millions of pipes as there be people under him."

§13. How can we leave the offices of *good neighborhood*,
without interposing a PROPOSAL, to animate and regulate PRI-
VATE MEETINGS *of religious people, for the exercises of religion?*
It is very certain, that where such *private meetings* under a good
conduct, have been kept alive, the Christians which have composed them, have like so many *coals of the altar* kept one another
alive, and kept up a lively Christianity in the neighborhood.
Such *societies* have been tried and strong engines, to uphold the

power of godliness. The throwing up of such *societies,* has been accompanied with a visible *decay of godliness;* the less *love* to them, the less *use* of them, there has been in a place, the less has *godliness* flourished there; the less there has been of, *the Kingdom of God.*[18]

The *rules* observed by some, ASSOCIATED FAMILIES, may be offered on this occasion with some advantage. They will tell us what *good* may be done by such *societies* in a neighborhood.

I. It is to be proposed, that about a dozen *families,* more or less, of a vicinity, agree to meet (the men and their wives) at each other's houses, once in a fortnight, or a month, at such a time as may be agreed upon, and spend a convenient quantity of time together, in the *exercises of religion.*

II. The *exercises of religion* proper for a *meeting,* are: for the brethren to begin and conclude with PRAYERS in their turns; for PSALMS to be sung; and for SERMONS to be repeated.

III. It were desirable, for the MINISTERS now and then, to afford their presence at the meeting, and *pray* with them, and *instruct* them, and *exhort* them, as they may see occasion.

IV. The *candidates* of the ministry may do well, to perform some of their *first services* here, and here shape and mold themselves for *further services.*

V. One special *design* of the *meeting,* should be, with *united prayers,* to ask the blessings of Heaven on the family where they are assembled, as well as on the rest: that with the wondrous force of *united prayers, two or three may agree on earth, to ask such things,* as are to be done for the families, by *our Father which is in Heaven.*

VI. Such a *meeting* should look upon themselves, as bound up in one *bundle of love;* and count themselves obliged, in very close and strong bonds, to be serviceable unto one another. If anyone in the society should fall into *affliction,* all the rest should presently study to relieve and support the afflicted person, in all the ways imaginable. If anyone should fall into *temp-*

tation, the rest should watch over him, and with the *spirit of meekness,* with the *meekness of wisdom,* endeavor to recover him. It should be like a *law of the Medes and Persians* to the whole society, that they will upon all just occasions, lovingly *give,* and as lovingly *take,* mutual admonitions of anything that they may see *amiss* in one another.

VII. And it is not easy to reckon up the *good offices,* that such a *society* may do to many, many others, as well as to the *members* whereof it is itself composed. The *prayers* of such well-disposed *societies,* may fetch down marvelous favors from Heaven on their *pastors,* whose *lives* may be prolonged, and *gifts* augmented, and *graces* brightened, and *labors* prospered, in answer to the supplications of such associated families; and the *interests of religion* may be mightily preserved and promoted in the *whole flock,* by their fervent supplications; and the *spirit of grace* mightily poured out upon the rising generation. Yea, *all the land* may fare the better for them.

VIII. Especially, when a *society* shall set apart *whole days* for *prayer* with *fasting* before the Lord, as it may be proper for them to do now and then upon some occasions. The *success* of such *days* has been sometimes very marvelous: and the *savor* of them, left on the minds of the saints, who have carried them on, has been such, as notably to prepare them, to *show forth the death of the Lord* at His Holy Table; yea, to *meet with their own death,* when God pleases to order it.

IX. It is very sure, the *devotions* first, and afterwards the *conferences,* carried on in such a *society,* will not only have a notable tendency to produce the *comfort of love* in the hearts of good men toward one another; but also their *abilities* will be thereby sharpened and quickened; they will be rendered more *able,* to serve many valuable interests.

X. Unexpected *opportunities to do good,* will arise unto such a *society:* but especially, if a practice of this importance were once taken up; that the MEN who compose the *society,* would now and then spend half an hour together by themselves, in considering on that question, WHAT GOOD IS THERE TO BE DONE?

More particularly:

Who are to be called upon, to do their duty, in coming to special ordinances?

Who is in any special adversity; and what shall be done to comfort them?

What contention or variance may there be among any neighbors, and what may be done for the healing of it?

What open miscarriages do any live in; and who shall be desired to carry faithful admonitions unto them?

Finally: What is there to be done for the advantage, and advancement of our holy religion?

In the primitive times of Christianity there was much use made of a saying, which they ascribed unto *Mathias* the Apostle: Εαν εκλεκτου Γειτων αμαρτηση, ημαρτεν ο εκλεκτος. *If the neighbor of an elect*, or godly, *man sin, the godly man himself has also sinned.* The obligations of neighbors watchfully to *admonish* one another, were what that saying intended. Oh! how much may *Christians associated* in religious combinations, do by watchful and faithful admonitions, to prevent being *partakers in other men's sins!*

The man, that shall produce, and promote such *societies*, will do an unknown deal of good in the *neighborhood.*

And so will he, that shall help forward another sort of SOCIETIES, namely, those of YOUNG MEN ASSOCIATED.

These duly managed, have been incomparable *nurseries* to the *churches*, where the faithful pastors have countenanced them. *Young men* are hereby *preserved* from very many *temptations*, rescued from the *paths of the Destroyer*, confirmed in the *right ways of the Lord*, and prepared mightily for such *religious ex-*

ercises as will be expected from them, when they come themselves to be *householders*.

I will make a tender of some ORDERS, which have been observed in some such *societies*.

I. Let there be *two hours* at a time set apart; and, let there
be *two prayers* made by the members of the *Society*, in their
turns; between which, let a *sermon* be repeated; and there may
be the singing of a *Psalm* annexed.

II. Let all the members of the Society, resolve to be *chari-
tably watchful* over one another: never to divulge one another's
infirmities; always to inform and advise one another of everything that may appear to call for an admonition, and to take it
kindly when they are admonished.

III. Let all who are to be admitted as members of the *Society*,
be accompanied by two or three of the rest, unto the *Minister*
of the place, that they may receive his holy counsels, and
charges, and that everything may be done with his approbation;
and so let their *names* be added unto the *roll*.

IV. If any person thus *enrolled* among them, fall into a
scandalous iniquity, let the rebukes of the *Society* be dispensed
unto him; and let them forbid him to come any more among
them, until he bring suitable expressions and evidences of *repentance* with him.

V. Let the *list* be once a quarter called over; and then, if it
be observed, that any of the *Society* have much absented themselves, let there be some sent unto them, to inquire the reason
of the absence; and if no reason be given, but such as intimates
an *apostasy* from good beginnings, let them upon obstinacy,
after loving and faithful admonitions, be obliterated.[19]

VI. Once in three months, let there be, if need be, a *collection*, out of which the necessary charges of the *Society* shall be
defrayed, and the rest be employed upon such pious uses, as may
be agreed upon.

VII. Once in *two months*, let the whole time of the meeting,

67

be devoted unto supplications, for the conversation and salvation of the *rising generation* in the land; and particularly, for the success of the Gospel, in that congregation, whereto the *Society* does belong.

VIII. Let the whole *Society*, be exceedingly careful, that their discourse while they are together, after the other services of religion are over, have nothing in it, that shall have any taint of *backbiting* or *vanity*, or the least relation to the affairs of *government*, or to things which do not concern them, and do not serve the interests of holiness in their own conversation. But let their discourse be wholly on the matters of religion; and those also, not the disputable and controversial matters, but the points of *practical piety*.[20] They may propose *questions* upon this intention, and everyone in an orderly manner, take his liberty to *answer* them. Or, they may go through the *Catechism*, and one at one time, another at another, hear all the rest recite the *answers* thereof. Or, they may otherwise be directed by their *pastors*, to spend their time together profitably.

IX. Let every person in the *Society*, look upon it, as a special task incumbent on him, to look out, for some other hopeful *young man*, and use all proper pains, to engage him in the resolutions of godliness, until he also shall be joined unto the *Society*. And when a *society* shall in this way be increased unto a fit number, let it *swarm* into *more;* who may hold an useful correspondence with one another.

The man, who shall be the instrument of setting up such a *society* in a place, cannot comprehend, unto what a long and rich train of good consequences, he is become instrumental.

And they that shall in such a *society* together carry on the duties of Christianity, and the praises of a glorious CHRIST, will have upon themselves, a blessed symptom, that they shall be together associated in the *Heavenly City*, and in the blessedness that shall never have an end.

[CHAPTER FOUR: MINISTERS]

§14. Hitherto my discourse has been a more *general address*, unto people of all conditions and capacities. I have proposed few *devices*, but those, upon which persons in *private* circumstances, as well as others, may be discoursed unto. We will proceed now to those that are in more *public* circumstances. And, first, because no men in the world are under such obligations to *do good*, as the MINISTERS OF THE GOSPEL, *it is necessary that the Word of God should be first spoken unto* THEM.

Will my fathers and brethren, give me leave. Certainly, they that are *men of God*, should be *always at work for God!* Certainly, they that are *dedicated* unto the special service of the Lord, should never be satisfied, but when they are in the most sensible manner serving Him. Certainly, they whom the *Great King* has brought nearer to Himself than other men, should be more unwearied than any men, in endeavors to advance His *Kingdom*. They whom the Word of God calls *angels*, ought certainly to be of an *angelical disposition;* disposed evermore to *do good*, like the *good angels; ministers* always on the wing to *do His pleasure.* 'Tis no improper PROPOSAL, that they would seriously set themselves to think, "What are the points wherein I should be wise and do good, like an angel of God?" Or, "If an angel were in flesh, as I am, and in such a post as I am, what methods may I justly imagine, he would use to glorify God?" What wonderful offices, of *kindness*, and with how much *delight*, would the *good angels* do, for such their *fellow-servants!* We must call upon our people, *to be ready to every good work.* We must go before them in it; by our own *readiness at every good work*, show them how. *Timothy, be thou an example of the believers!* It is a true maxim, and you cannot think too often upon it: "The life of a minister, is the life of his ministry." And there is another maxim like unto it: "The sins of teachers are the teachers of sins."

Allow me, Sirs. Your *opportunities to do good*, are singular. Your want of wordly *riches*, and of any way ordinarily to get 'em, is compensated by the *opportunities to do good*, which you are *enriched* withal. The true *spirit of a minister*, will cause you to count yourselves *enriched*, when those precious things are conferred upon you, and to prize them above any *farms*, or *bags*, or whatever temporal possessions.

*In operibus sit abundantia mea; Divitiis per me licet, abundet, quisquis voluerit.** Well struck, brave *Melanchthon!* [1]

'Tis to be hoped, that the main principle that acted you, when you first entered upon the *evangelical ministry*, was, **an** *hope to do good in the world.* If that principle were then too feeble in its operation, 'tis time that it should now operate, and that you should now vigorously act upon it, and that the *zeal* thereof should now *eat up* your time, your thought, your all.

That you may be *good men*, and be mightily inspired and assisted from Heaven to *do good*, it is needful that you should be *men of prayer*. I lay this down to be allowed, as my very first *postulatum!* In the pursuance of this intention, there appears more than a little need of it, that you should ever now and then keep whole *days of prayer*, in an holy retirement before the Lord; often set apart, whole *days*, for *prayer with fasting*, in secret, and perfume your studies with *devotions extraordinary:* and usually with a mixture of *alms*, to go up in the *memorial* before the Lord.[2] By such *days*, you may obtain, with the pardon of your *unfruitfulness*, for which, alas, how often have we cause to repair unto the Great *Sacrifice!*—you may obtain, I say, a vast improvement in *piety* and *sanctity;* which is, of how vast consequence, to make an *useful minister!* *Sanctify them in* (or for) *thy truth*,[3] says our Saviour. They should

* My wealth is in good works; let anyone who wishes, be rich.

70

be *sanctified,* that would be instruments for the propagation of the *truth.* You may obtain, a certain *afflatus* from Heaven upon your minds, and such an *indwelling of the Holy Spirit,* as will render you, grave, discreet, humble, generous, and *men* worthy to be *greatly beloved.* You may obtain those influences from above, that will dispel the *enchantments,* and conquer the *temptations,* which may else do a world of mischief in your neighborhood. You may obtain *direction* and *assistance* from Heaven, for the many services to be done, in your discharge of your ministry. Finally, you may fetch down unknown *blessings* on your flocks, and the whole people for which you are to be *the Lord's remembrancers.*

Your *public prayers* well composed and well adapted, will be excellent *engines* to *do good.* The more judicious, the more affectionate, the more argumentative, you are in them, the more you will *teach your people to pray.* Yea, I beseech you, Sirs; how can you prosecute any *intention of piety* among your people more effectually, than by letting them see you praying, and weeping, and striving, and in an importunate agony before the Lord, that you may gain it for them?

The more significantly you represent the *various cases* of your people in your *public prayers;* the more devoutly sensible you will make them of their own cases. And it will wonderfully comfort them!

The *prayers* made at *baptisms,* may be so managed, as mightily to awaken in all people, the conscience of their baptismal obligations.

What effusions of the *Holy Spirit,* may your people feel, if your prayers at the *Table* of the Lord, are, as *Nazianzen* I remember says, his Fathers' were; *made by the Holy Spirit of God!*

Your *sermons,* if they be *well-studied,* as from the consideration of their being *offerings* unto God, *the Great* KING, as well as unto His people, they ought to be, will *do good* beyond all expression. The manner of your *studying* them, is that which may much contribute unto it. It is needful, that you study the *condition* of your flocks; and bring them such *truths*, as will notably *suit* their present circumstances. In order to this, you will observe their *condition*, their faults, their snares, their griefs, that you may *speak a word in season;* and if anything remarkable fall out, you will suit the *words* to the *works* of God. You may divide your people into *classes;* and think, what lessons of piety you are to dispense, unto the *communicants;* what, unto all that are under the *bonds of the Covenant;* what, unto the *aged;* what unto the *worldly;* what unto the *rich;* what unto the *poor;* what unto them that are in *offices;* what unto them that are under such, and such *afflictions;* what in regard of people's *personal callings.* Above all, the *young* must not be forgotten: you will employ all the *tunes* imaginable, to raise *early piety.* Yea, you may do well to let it be understood, that you would willingly be advised, by any *persons,* or *meetings,* in your flocks, what *subjects* they may want or wish to hear treated on; by giving them *sermons* on such *subjects,* you at least very much edify those who have asked for them; and it is probable, very many more.

And, what if while you are studying your *sermons,* you should at the close of every paragraph, make a *pause,* and endeavor with *acknowledgments* and *ejaculations* to Heaven, and with *self-examinations,* to feel some impressions of the *truths* in that paragraph on your own souls, before you go any further? By such a practice, the *hours* which you take, to make and write a *sermon,* will prove so many *hours of devotion* with you. The *day* in which you have made a *sermon* will even leave upon your mind, such a savor as a *day of prayer* uses to do. When you come to preach the sermon, you will do it with great liberty and assurance; and the *truths* thus prepared will be likely to come with a more sensible warmth and life upon the auditory: *from the heart, and to the heart!* A famous preacher would say, "I never durst preach a sermon to others, till I have got first some good by it myself." And I will add, *That is the way for it to do much good unto others.* Let such a *rabbi*, be called, our *Hadarsan!* (or, the *preacher!*) Let the saying of the ancient be remembered: *Qui ludit in cathedra lugebit in Gehenna.*† And the saying of a modern also, not be forgotten: *Cold preachers make bold sinners.*

But then, Sirs, your VISITS; Oh! how much may you do for CHRIST among your people in them! It is pity but that you should impose it as a law upon yourselves: *never to make an unprofitable visit.* Even when you render a pure *visit* of *civility*, or for *diversion*, 'tis easy for you, to keep this law: *that you will drop some speech or other, good for the use of edifying, before you leave the company.* There have been *pastors* able to say, they scarce ever once went into an house among their people in their lives, without some essay or purpose to *do good* in the house, before they came out of it.[4]

The same rule would be very well observed with such as *come* unto us, as well as with those whom we *go* unto. Why should any of our people ever come anear us, without our contriving, *to speak something to them that may be useful to them!* Our *Peter Martyr* having been many days in *Bucer's* house, published this report of it:[5] *Ausim affirmare, me ab illius mensa, semper discessisse Doctiorem.*‡ I make no doubt, that the observation of this rule, may be very consistent with an *affable*, yea, and, as far as is *convenient*, a *facetious* conversation. Though *Quae sunt in ore populi nugae, sunt in ore sacerdotis blasphemiae.*§

But, Sirs, in your *visits*, you will take a particular notice of

† He who trifles in the pulpit will lament in hell.
‡ I always came away from that man's table a wiser man.
§ The people's trifles, when spoken by the priest, are blasphemies.

the *widow*, the *orphan*, the *afflicted;* and carry all agreeable reliefs unto them. The *bills* put up in your congregations, will a little help you, to find out, who need your *visits*.

If any *special calamity* hath befallen anyone, 'tis a time to *visit* them, with very particular *directions* and *persuasions* unto them, to hear the *voice of God* in the calamity; to comply with the *intent* and *errand*, which it comes upon.

If anyone has received any *special deliverance*, 'tis a time to *visit* them, and therein to persuade them, that they will think of some *singular thing*, to be done by way of thankfulness for their deliverance; and not leave them, till the thing be agreed and resolved upon.

The *handmaids of the Lord*, that are near their *lying in*, may on this account be very proper objects for your *visits*. At such a time they are in much distress; the approaching *hour of trouble* threatens to be their *dying hour*. The counsels that will exactly instruct them how to prepare for a *dying hour*, will now if ever, be attentively hearkened unto. And there are precious *promises* of God, which they should also be taught now to live upon. To bring them these *promises* will do the work, and give you the welcome, of a *good angel* unto them.

CATECHIZING, is a noble exercise; it will insensibly bring you into a way to *do good*, that surpasses all expression. Your *sermons* will be very much lost upon an *uncatechized people*. Nor will your people mind so much, what you speak to them in the pulpit, as what you speak to them in the more *approaching* and *familiar* way, of applying the answers of the *catechism*. Never any *minister*, that was a *great catechizer* did repent of it; thousands, thousands! have blessed God, with wonders and praises, for the good success of it. The most *honorable man of God* should reckon it, no abasement or abatement of his honor, to stoop unto this *way of teaching*. Yea, some eminent pastors, in their emerited *old age*, when other labors have been too hard for them, have, like the famous old *Gerson*,[6] wholly given themselves up to *catechizing;* though there have been others of whom that brave Chancellor of *Paris,* in his treatise, *De Pueris ad Christum trahendis,*|| makes a sad complaint: *Adeo jam indignum videtur apud multos, si quis ex theologis, aut famatus in literis, vel ecclesiastica dignitate praeditus, ad hoc opus se inclinaverit.*¶

The methods of carrying on this exercise, will be varied by the *pastors,* who so *love* a glorious CHRIST, as to mind His Word, *Feed my lambs;* according to the varieties of their circumstances.

But some have chosen the way of PASTORAL VISITS. And from the memorials of one who long since did so, and then left his PATERNA to his *son* upon it, I will transcribe the ensuing passages.[7]

For, PASTORAL VISITS

"You may set upon *visiting* all the families, belonging to your flock; taking *one afternoon* in a week for that purpose.

"You may still send beforehand unto the *families,* that you intend at such a time to *visit* them. And when you come unto them; you may assay with as handsome and as pungent addresses as you are able, to treat every person particularly about their everlasting interests.

"First. You may discourse with the *elder* people upon such points as you think most proper for them.

"And especially, charge them to maintain *family prayer;* and obtain their promises for it, if they have yet neglected. Yea, now *pray with them,* that you may show them *how to pray,* as well as to obtain their purposes for it.

"You may likewise press upon them, the care of instructing their *children* and *servants,* in the holy religion of our *Saviour;* and to bring them up for Him.

"If any that you should have spoken with, were absent, you

|| On Bringing Children to Christ.

¶ To many people it seems unworthy for theologians, noted men of letters, or leaders of the church to like this work.

may frequently leave a solemn text or two of the *Sacred Scripture*, which you think most agreeable for them; desiring somebody present, that they would remember you kindly to them, and from you recommend unto them *that Oracle* of God.

"You may then call for the *children* and *servants;* and putting unto them such *questions* of the *Catechism*, as you think fit, you may, from the *answers*, make as lively applications unto them, as you can, for the engaging of them unto the fear of God.

"You may frequently get *promises* from them, relating to *secret prayer*, and *reading* of the *Scriptures*, and *obedience* to their *parents* and *masters*.

"And you may frequently set before them the *proposals* of the *New Covenant*, after you have labored for their conviction and awakening; till with floods of tears, they expressly declare their consenting to, and accepting of, the *proposals* of the *Covenant of Grace*, which you distinctly set before them.

"Some of the *lesser folks*, you may order, to bring their *Bibles* unto you, and read unto you from thence two or three verses, whereto you may turn them. This will *try*, whether they can *read well*, or no. You may then charm them to think on such things, as you thence observe for their admonition, and never forget those *faithful sayings* of God.

"You may sometimes leave some *awful question* with them; which, you may tell them, they shall not answer to *you*, but answer to *themselves*. As, 'What have I been doing, ever since I came into the world, about the great errand upon which God sent me into the World?' And, 'If God should now call me out of the world, what would become of me throughout eternal ages?' And, 'Have I ever yet by faith carried a perishing soul unto my only Saviour, for both righteousness and salvation?'

"You will enjoy a most wonderful presence of God with you, in this undertaking; and seldom leave a *family*, without many *tears* of devotion dropt by all sorts of persons in it.

"You can seldom dispatch more than *four* or *five* families in

76

an afternoon; and the work may be as *laborious* as any in all your ministry.

"*My son*, I advise you, to set a special value upon that part of your ministry, which is to be discharged in PASTORAL VISITS. You will not only *do*, but also *get*, more than a little good, by your conversation with all sorts of persons, in thus *visiting* of them *from house to house*. And you will never more *walk in the spirit*, than when you thus *walk* about your flock, to do what good you can among them."

In your *visits*, an incredible deal of good may be done, by distributing little *books of piety*. You may without *great cost*, be furnished with *little books* to suit all occasions: *books* for the *old*, and for the *young; books* for persons under *afflictions*, or under *desertions; books* for persons under the power of special *vices; books* for them that neglect *household piety; books* for the *sea-faring; books* for the *erroneous; books* for them whom you would quicken and prepare to approach the *Table* of the Lord; *books* for them that come to have their children *baptized*. And *catechisms* for the ignorant. You may notably clench your admonitions, by leaving agreeable *books* in the hands of those, whom you have discoursed withal; you may give them to know, that you would be looked upon as discoursing by *these* unto them, after you are departed from them. And in this way you may speak more than you have time to speak in any personal interview: yea, sometimes more than you would care to speak. By good *books*, there is a *salt of piety* scattered about a neighborhood.

Pastors, uphold and cherish good *schools* in your towns. But then, be prevailed withal sometimes to *visit* the *schools*.

It is a proposal made, by holy Mr. *Thomas White; that able and zealous ministers, might sometimes preach at the schools. Because the preaching of the Word is the converting ordinance; and the children will be obliged there to hear with more attention than they often do in the public. And the ministers might here condescend unto such expressions, as might work most upon them, and such as are not so fit for a public congregation.* I have read this account of one who was awakened by this Advice, to do such things as these.[8]

"At certain times he successively visited the *schools*. When he came to a *school*, he first made a *prayer* over the *children*, as much adapted unto their condition, as he could make it. Then he went through the *Catechism;* or as much of it, as he thought necessary; making the several *children* to repeat the several *answers*. But he still broke the *questions*, for each article in the *answers*, to be understood by them, with a *Yes*, or *No*, expected from them. And he put such *questions* also, as would make them to see and own their own *duties*, and often to express a resolution to do their *duties*. Then he preached a short *sermon* to them; exceeding plain; on some suitable Scripture; and with all the artifice and pungency he could use, to raise attention and affection in them. After this he singled out a number of *scholars*, it may be seven or eight, or ten; and bid each of them turn to a certain Scripture; which he made them read unto the whole *school;* because it still related unto something as he gave them to see by his brief remarks upon it, which it particularly concerned children to take notice of. Then he concluded with a brief *prayer*, for a blessing on the *school*, and on the *tutors* in it."

We are upon *visiting;* you will be sure to *visit* the *poor* as well as the *rich;* and often mention the condition of the *poor*, in your conversation with the *rich*. Keep, Sir, a *list* of 'em!

And think on this, the *wind* feeds nobody, yet it may turn the *mill*, which will grind the *corn*, that may feed the *poor*. In talking with the *rich*, you may do this for the *poor* in your *list*.

But then, in visiting the *poor*, you will take occasion to dispense your *alms* among them. These *alms* you will, with as much contrivance as may be, make the *vehicles*, to convey the *admonitions of piety* unto them; yea, the methods and machines

78

of obtaining from them, some engagements to perform certain *exercises of piety.* All ministers are not alike *furnished* for *alms;* they should all be *disposed* for them. They that have *small families,* or *large interests,* ought to be shining examples of liberality to the poor, and pour down their *alms* like the showers of Heaven upon them. Yet *all* should endeavor to *do what they can* this way. What says *Nazianzen* of his reverend fathers' *alms-deeds?* They will find, that the more they *do* (provided it be *done with discretion*), the more they *may;* the *loaves* will multiply in the *distribution.* Sirs, this bounty of yours to the *poor,* will procure a mighty esteem and success to your ministry. *Suadet lingua, jubet vita.** 'Twill be an ungainsayable demonstration, that you *believe what you speak,* about all the duties of *Christianity,* but particularly of *liberality,* and a *faithful discharge of our stewardship,* and a mind weaned from the *love of this world;* it will demonstrate your belief of a *future state.* It will vindicate you from the imputation of, *a worldly man;* it will embolden you, and fortify you, with a great assurance, when you call upon others, *to do good,* and abound in the *sacrifices* which *God is well-pleased* withal. *Et sic exempla parantur!†*

You will do well to keep a watchful eye on the *disorders* that may grow up and get head, in your neighborhood. Among other ways to suppress those things, you may form *Societies for the Suppression of Disorders;* obtain a fit number of prudent, pious, well-affected men, to *associate* upon that intention; employ *their* discretion, and *their* activity, for your assistance in your holy purposes.

One of the rules given for the *minister,* is, *Give thyself to reading.* Sirs, let *Gregory's Pastoral,* and *Bowles's Pastor Evangelicus,* be some of the books on which you bestow a *reading.*[9] But then, if you read *Church History* very much (and particu-

---

* The tongue advises, the life commands.
† Thus are examples given!

larly, the *Prudentia Veteris Ecclesiae*,‡ written by *Vedelius*),[10] but especially the *lives* of both ancient and modern *divines*, you will ever now and then find, *methods to do good*, exemplified. You will then consider, how far you may *go and do likewise*.

How serviceable may *ministers* be, unto one another, and unto all the churches, in their several *associations!* Many things of general advantage to all their flocks may be advanced, and consulted there. Yea, 'tis pity, that there should be the least occasional *meeting of ministers* at any time, without *some useful thing* proposed in it.

Nero took it very ill, that *Vespasian* slept, at his *music!* It is very much, very much to be wished, that the sin of *sleeping at sermons*, were more watched against, and more warned against. Your *sleepy hearers*, if, alas, the *catachresis* may be allowed that calls them *hearers*, do miserably lose the *good* of your ministry; and the *good* which you might, perhaps, have particularly designed for them, whom at the time of your speaking what you prepared for them, you see seized with an horrible *spirit of slumber* before your eyes. Will no *vinegar* help against the *narcotics*, that Satan has given to your poor *Eutychus's!* [11] Or, can't you bring that *civility* into fashion among your hearers, *to wake one another!*

Finally, after all the generous essays and labors to *do good*, that may fill your lives, your people will probably treat you with much *ingratitude*. Your *salaries* will be meaner than even those at *Geneva*. They will *neglect* you; they will *oppress* you; they will *defraud* you, of what they have engaged, and you have expected. You have now one opportunity more to *do good*, and so to glorify your Saviour. Your *patience*, O tried servants of God, your *patience* will do it wonderfully! To *bear evil* is to *do good*. The more *patient* you are under *ill usage*, the more you exhibit a glorious CHRIST unto your people, in your conformity to your admirable Saviour. The more *conformed* you

‡ The Prudence of the Ancient Church.

are unto Him, the more *prepared* you are, 'tis possible, for some amendment of your condition in this world; most certainly for the recompenses of the Heavenly world, when you appear before the Lord, who says, "I know thy works, and charity, and service, and faith, and thy patience." [12]

I will say this: If to represent, a glorious CHRIST, unto the view, and love, and admiration of all people, be the grant [grand?] intention of your *lives;* to be a *star* that leads men to Christ, and stands there! (Ο τον χρισον εν τη ψυχη περιφερων,§ was the character, you know, of *Ignatius!*) [13] if you are exquisitely studious, that the *holiness*, and yet the *gentleness*, of a glorious CHRIST may shine in your conversation: if in your *public* discourses you do with rapture bring in the mention of a glorious CHRIST in every paragraph, on every occasion, where He is to be spoken of; and in your *private* ones, you contrive to insinuate something of His *glories* and *praises*, wherever it may be decently introduced; lastly, if when you find that a glorious CHRIST is the more considered and acknowledged by your means, it fills you with wonderful satisfaction; and with *joy unspeakable and full of glory*, you now cry out, "Lord, this is my desired happiness!" Truly, Sirs, you then *live to purpose;* you *do good* emphatically!

There was a worthy minister whom the great *Cranmer* [14] designed for preferment; and he gave this account of his design about him: *Nihil appetit, nihil ardet, nihil somniat, nisi* JESUM CHRISTUM.|| Verily, such *men of Christ*, are *men of God*. They are the *favorites of Heaven;* and shall be *favored* with opportunities to *do good*, above any men in the world: they are the *men whom the King of Heaven will delight to honor!* And they are the *Gaons* [15] of Christianity.

If I reserve one thing to be mentioned after *Finally*, 'tis

§ he who carries Christ in his heart.

|| He desires nothing, yearns for nothing, dreams of nothing but Jesus Christ.

because I am in a doubt, whether it should be mentioned at all. In some *Reformed churches*, they do not permit a *minister* of the Gospel, to practice as a *physician*, because either of those callings is ordinarily enough to find a full employment for him that faithfully follows it. But, the *priests* of old, who reserved in the archives of their temples, the stories of the cures thankfully acknowledged there, communicated from thence directions for cures in such cases among their neighbors. Nor has it been a rare thing in later ages for *clergymen* to be *physicians*. Not only such monks as *Ægidius Atheniensis*, and *Constantinus Afer*, and others, who had leisure for it; but such bishops as *Bochelt*, yea, such archbishops as *Albicus*, have appeared under that character.[16] So, *Herbert* [17] advises that his *Country Minister* (or at least, his wife) should be much of a *physician* to his flock. And we have known many a *country minister* prove a vast blessing to his flock, by being so. If a *minister* do anything this way, let him forever make it an engine, to address the *souls* of his people, and oblige them unto piety. 'Tis an *angelical conjunction*, when *the ministers who do the pleasure* of CHRIST, shall also be *physicians* and *Raphaels* [18] unto their people! In a more *populous place*, you will perhaps choose rather, Sir, to get some religious and accomplished *physician* into your neighborhood; and make *medical studies* your own diversion as much as may be; but with some eye to this, that you will communicate unto your *Luke*,[19] what notable things you do in reading meet withal; and sometimes *unite counsels* with him, for the good of his patients. You may this way save the *lives* of many, who may themselves know nothing of it.

[CHAPTER FIVE: SCHOOLMASTERS]

§15. From the Tribe of *Levi*, we will pass with our PROPOSALS to the Tribe of *Simeon:* [1] from which latter *tribe*, there has been a frequent *ascent* into the former; as well as a step now and then from the former to the latter. The SCHOOLMASTER has manifold *opportunities* to *do good*. God make him sensible of his *obligations!* We read, *The little ones have their angels*. It is an *hard* work to keep a *school*. But it is a *good* work; and it may be so done, as to be in some sort like the *work of angels*. The *tutors* of the children, may be like their *tutelar angels. Melchior Adam* [2] did well to call it, *Molestissimam, sed Deo longe gratissimam functionem.*¶

Tutors, will you not look upon the *children* under your wing as committed unto you, by the glorious LORD, with a charge of this importance: *Take them, and bring them up for me, and I will pay you your wages!* Every time any new children come under your tuition, why should you not think: "Here, my Glorious Lord sends me another object, on which I may do something, that He may be served in the world!" O *suffer little children to come unto* you, and consider, what you may do, that *of such may be the Kingdom of Heaven!*

Sirs, let it be a great intention with you, *to instil documents of piety into the children*. Esteem it, your and their great interest, that they should so *know the Holy Scriptures as to be made wise unto salvation*, and *know the Saviour, whom to know is life eternal*. Oh! take all occasions to drop some *honey out of the rock* upon them! Happy the *children*, and as happy the *master*, where they who make the Relation [3] of their conversion to serious piety, may say, "There was a schoolmaster that

¶ A most troublesome office, but most pleasing to God.

83

brought us to CHRIST!" You have been told: "Certainly, 'tis a nobler work, to make the little ones know their *Saviour*, than to know their *letters*. The lessons of *Jesus* are nobler things than the lessons of *Cato*. A sanctifying *transformation* of their souls, were a nobler thing, than merely to construe *Ovid's Metamorphosis*. He was a good *Schoolmaster*, of whom there was this testimony given.

> Young *Austin* wept, when he saw *Dido* dead;
> Though not a tear for a *dead soul* he had.
> Our Master would not let us be so vain,
> But us from *Virgil* did to *David* train.
> *Textor's* epistles would not *clothe* our souls;
> *Paul's* too we learnt; we *went to school at Paul's*."

CATECHIZING; that should be a *frequent*, and at least, a *weekly*, exercise of the *school*. And in the most *edifying*, and *applicatory* and *admonitory* manner carried on. "In some reformed places (we are told) the Magistrate countenances none to keep a *school*, but what appears with a *testimonial* of their *ability*, and their *disposition* particularly (*Aptitudinis ad munus illud imprimis puerorum catechisationem*) for the work of *religious catechizing*."

Dr. *Reynolds*,[4] in a funeral sermon on an eminent *schoolmaster* has a passage worthy to be written in letters of gold. "If *grammar schools* have *holy* and *learned* men set over them, not only the *brains*, but also the *souls* of the children might be there enriched, and the work of *learning* and of *grace* too, be betimes wrought in them." In order to this, 'tis to be proposed, that you would not only *pray* with your scholars every day, but also take occasion from the *public sermons*, and from *remarkable occurrences* of Providence in your neighborhood, often to inculcate the *lessons of piety* upon the children.

Tutors in the *College*, may do well successively to treat each of their *pupils* alone, with all possible solemnity and affection, about their *interior state;* show them how to repent of *sin*, and believe on *Christ;* and bring them to express *resolutions* of *serious piety.* Sirs, you may do a thousand things, to render your *pupils orthodox* in their principles, *regular* in their practices, *qualified* for services!

I have read this experiment of one who had *pupils* under his charge: "He made it his custom, that in every *recitation,* he would, from something or other occurring in it, *make an occasion,* to let fall some *sentence,* which had a tendency to promote the *fear of God* in their hearts; which thing sometimes did indeed put him to more than a little study; but the good effect sufficiently recompensed it." [5]

If I should press for certain authors to be made classical in the *grammar schools,* which are not commonly used there; such as *Castalio* for the *Latin* tongue, and *Posselius* for the Greek; [6] or, if I should beg, with certain modern writers, "That there may be a *Northwest Passage* found, for the attaining of the *Latin tongue;* that instead of a journey which may be dispatched in a few days, they may not wander, like the Children of *Israel,* many years in the wilderness": or, if I should recite *Austin's* complaints, of little boys learning the filthy actions of the pagan gods in the schools, for giving an account whereof, says he, *Ob hoc bonae spei puer appellabar;* * and *Luther's,* that our *schools* are more *pagan* than *Christian;* and the reports and wishes of a late writer, who says: "I knew an aged and famous *schoolmaster,* that after he had kept school about fifty years, said with a sad countenance, that it was a great trouble unto him, that he spent so much time in reading pagan authors to his scholars, and wished it were customary to read such a book as *Duport's* verses upon *Job,*[7] rather than *Homer,* and such books. I pray God, put it in the hearts of a wise Parliament, to *purge our schools;* that instead of learning vain fictions, and filthy stories, they may be acquainted with the Word of God, and with books containing grave sayings, and things that may make them truly wise and

* I was called a boy of great promise.

useful in the world": I suppose, there will be little notice taken of such *proposals:* I had as good never mention them; 'tis with *despair,* that I make mention of them.

Among the *occasions* to be taken for instilling of *piety* into the *scholars,* there is one peculiarly at the *writing schools.* An inveterate sinner I have read of, converted unto serious piety, by accidentally seeing that *sentence* of *Austin* written in a window: "He that hath promised pardon to the penitent sinner, has not promised repentance to the presumptuous one." Who can tell what good may be done to the young scholar, by a *sentence* in a *copy-book?* Let their *copies* be of *sentences* worthy to be *had in everlasting remembrance;* of *sentences,* that shall have the brightest *maxims of wisdom* in them; worthy to be written on the *fleshy tables* of their hearts; to be graven with the *point of a diamond* there. This may do two executions *with one stone:* God has blessed this unto many *scholars,* it has done them good all their days.

At the *grammar school* also, the scholars may be ordered for their exercises to turn such things into *Latin,* as may be likewise for their instruction and establishment, in the principles of Christianity; and render them armed with *supplies from the Tower of David.* Their *epistles,* why may they not be on such *subjects* as may most befriend virtue in them!

I will add this: To carry on the *discipline of the school,* with *rewards,* as well as *punishments,* is most certainly very *advisable,* very *preferable.* There may be invented many ways of *rewarding,* the *diligent* and the *laudable:* and—*ad palmae cursurus honores* †—a child of any ingenuity, under the *expectations* and *encouragements* of being *rewarded,* will do to the uttermost. You have an honor for *Quintilian.*[8] I pray, hear *Quintilian: Cavendum a plagis, sed potius laude, aut aliorum praelatione, urgendus est puer.*‡ If a fault must be *punished,* let *instruction,*

† running after the honors of victory.
‡ The boy must be encouraged by praise rather than frightened of flogging.

86

both unto the *delinquent* and unto the *spectator*, accompany the *correction*. Let the *odious nature* of the *sin*, that has enforced the *correction*, be declared; and let nothing be done in a *passion;* all be done with all the evidence of *compassion* that may be.

Ajax Flagellifer [9] may be read at the school. He is not fit for to be the master of it. Let it not be said of the scholars, "They are brought up *in the School of Tyrannus.*" *Pliny* [10] says, that *bears* are the fatter for beating. Fitter to have the conduct of *bears* than of ingenuous *boys*, are the masters, that can't give a *bit* of learning, but they must give a *knock* with it. Send 'em to be tutors of the famous *Lithuanian* school, at *Samourgan.*[11] The harsh, fierce, *Orbilian* [12] way of treating the children, too commonly used in the *school*, is a dreadful *curse* of God upon our miserable offspring, who are *born children of wrath.* It is boasted now and then of a *schoolmaster*, that such and such a *brave man* had his education under him. There is nothing said, how many that might have been *brave men*, have been destroyed by him; how many *brave wits*, have been dispirited, confounded, murdered, by his *barbarous* way of managing them.

I have read an address of this importance, and I will conclude with it, as one of great importance.

TUTORS, be *strict;* but yet be *gentle* too;
Don't by fierce *cruelties* fair *hopes* undo.
Dream not, that they who are to learning slow
Will mend by arguments in *ferio.*[13]
Who keeps the *golden fleece*, oh, let him not
A *dragon* be, tho' he *three tongues* have got.
Why can you not to learning find the way,
But thro' the Province of *Severia?*
'Twas *Moderatus* who taught *Origen;*
A *youth* which proved one of the best of men.
The lads with *honor* first, and *reason*, rule;
Blows are but for the *refractory fool.*
But, oh! first teach them their great God to fear;
An *Euge*,[14] so from God and them you'll hear.

[CHAPTER SIX: CHURCHES]

§16. We have lately discoursed with the PASTORS, about several ways to *do good*. There are PROPOSALS, to be also laid before the CHURCHES, of matters wherein they may do well to join with their *pastors*.

DAYS OF PRAYER kept now and then by the *churches*, on the declared intention of obtaining the *sanctifying influences* of the Spirit of Grace upon the rising generation, have had and would have, a marvelous efficacy to produce a *religious posterity* in the land; and a *seed accounted unto the Lord for a generation*. Such an acknowledgment of *supernatural grace* in the necessity and excellency of it, would be a very probable *preparative* and *introduction*, to the communication of it. And when the *children* see their *parents* thus earnestly seeking the *grace* of God for them, it would have a *natural tendency* to awaken them, unto an earnest seeking of it for themselves. The *sermons* also preached by the ministers on such solemn occasions, 'tis likely, would be very awakening ones. That this PROPOSAL, has been so little hearkened unto, 'tis lamentable, 'tis admirable! But—*They all slumbered and slept.*[1]

There is another PROPOSAL, which has been tendered to all our churches, and attended in some of them.

"That the several churches, having in an *instrument* proper for that purpose, made a *catalogue* [2] of such things, as can indisputably be found amiss among them, do with all seriousness and solemnity pass their VOTES, that they count such things to be very *offensive evils*, and that renouncing all dependence on their own strength, to avoid such evils, they humbly ask the help of the *Divine Grace*, to assist them in watching against the said evils, both in themselves and in one another. And that the *communicants* do often reflect upon those their Acknowledgments and Protestations, as perpetual Monitors unto them, to prevent the miscarriages wherewith too many professors a. too easily overtaken.'

It has been considered, t at such humble *recognitions of duty*, will not only be accepted by our God, as our *declarations* for Him, whereupon He will declare for us; but also, they are the *way of the New Covenant*, for our obtaining of help to do our duty.

A particular *church*, may be an illustrious *pillar of truth*, by considering what laboring *truth*, and *part* of the Kingdom of God, may call for special, signal, open Testimonies; and they may excite their *pastors* to the composing, and assist them in the publishing, of such *testimonies;* and appear to accompany them in the action. It is likely, that God would accompany such *testimonies* with a marvelous efficacy to suppress growing *errors* and *evils!*

A Proposal of this nature may be worthy of some consideration.

I. "It were to be desired, that every *particular church*, would be furnished with a Stock, that may be a constant and ready Fund for the Propagation of Religion. And that every minister would use his best endeavors, both with his own disbursements according to his ability, and with his applications unto well-disposed people under his influences, to increase the Stock; either in the way of *collections* publicly made at certain periods, or in the way of more private communications made from time to time unto it.

II. "This Evangelical Treasury may be lodged in the hands of the *deacons* of each of the churches, where it is gathered; who are to keep true and fair accounts of all that is brought in and laid out. And let nothing be drawn out of it, without the knowledge and consent of the *church*, to which it belongs.

III. "The first and main intention of this Evangelical

Treasury, is to be, *the propagation of religion.* And therefore, when any essays of good are to be made upon *ungospellized places,* the neighboring ministers may advise each of the churches, what *proportion* they may allow out of their Evangelical Treasury, towards the support of such a noble undertaking.

IV. "But this Evangelical Treasury may be capable of being applied unto some other *pious uses;* and particularly, unto such as any *particular church* may see cause to pursue, for the service of religion, within their own vicinity. Such as, the sending of *Bibles,* and *Catechisms,* and other *instruments of piety,* to be dispersed among the poor, where it may be thought necessary. Moreover, the help of new congregations abroad, in their first essays, to build *meeting houses* for the public worship of God with Scriptural purity; may be one article of expense for this Evangelical Treasury."

Quaere. Our churches have their *sacramental collections.* 'Tis not fit indeed, that they should be without them. The primitive Christians had so. *Justin Martyr* tells us of the τα συλλεξομενα; § *Tertullian* speaks of the *deposita pietatis,*|| on these occasions. May not our churches do well to augment their liberality, in their grateful and joyful *collections* at the Table of the Lord, and resolve, that what is now collected, shall be part of their Evangelical Treasury; not only, for their supply of the *Table,* and for the relief of the *poor,* but also for such *other services* to the Kingdom of God, as they may from time to time, see cause to countenance?

§ collections
|| deposits of piety.

[CHAPTER SEVEN: MAGISTRATES]

§17. From *ecclesiastical* circumstances, which in such a subject as we are now upon, may with good heraldry claim the *precedency*, we will make a transition to *political*. Now, *touch the mountains, and they will smoke!* Oh! when will *wisdom* visit *princes and nobles*, and all the *judges of the earth;* and inspire them to preserve the due lustre of their character, by a desire to *do good in the earth;* a study to *glorify the God of Heaven!* The opportunities that RULERS have to *do good,* are so evident, so numerous, and they have so much *power to do good,* that he who addresses them, cannot but be overwhelmed with some confusion of thought, where to begin, or when to conclude, or how to assign a fit order unto them. Indeed the very definition of government, is, *a care of other people's safety*. Sirs, from whom have you received this *power?* You could have *no power at all, except it were given you from above.* Certainly what is thus *received* from God, should be *employed* for God. *Be wise now therefore,* O ye rulers, *be instructed, ye judges of the earth. Serve the Lord, with fear,* lest ye forget and offend Him, who has made you what you are. *Kiss the feet of the Son of God, lest He be displeased* at your neglect of your duty. Don't *kindle the wrath* of Him who is, *the blessed and only Potentate, the King of Kings, and Lord of Lords.* What is the name of a MAGISTRATE? The name which He that made him, has given him, is: *the minister of God for good.* His *empty name* will produce a *cruel crime,* if he don't set himself to *do good,* as far as ever he can extend his influences. Is he a *vice-regent* of *God,* and shall he do nothing for *God?* Gross absurdity! Black ingratitude! Is he one of those whom the word of God coming to them has called, *gods? Gods* who *do no good*, are strange *gods*. Not *gods*, but another name, too horrible to be mentioned belongs unto them: shall we say, "Gods that have mouths but they speak not: eyes but they see not: noses but they smell not, and hands but they handle not"? *Government* is called, *the ordinance of God*. As the administration of it, is to avoid those *illegalities*, which will render it no other than a *violation* of the *ordinance;* thus it should vigorously pursue those noble and blessed *ends* for which it is *ordained; the good of mankind.* Unworthy of all their other flourishing *titles,* be they what they will, are the *rulers,* who are not ambitious of that above all: to be entitled *benefactors.* The greatest monarch in Christendom; one that by computation has fourscore millions of subjects, and he whom the Scripture styles, *the head over many countries,* is in the sacred prophecies called, *a vile person.* Verily, so is every *magistrate,* who does not aim to *do good in the world. Rulers* who make no other use of their higher station, than to swagger over their neighbors, and command their obsequious flatteries, and enrich themselves with the spoils of which they are able to pillage them, and then wallow in sensual and brutal pleasures; these are, *the basest of men.* From a sense of this, the *Venetians* though they allow concubines, yet if a man be observably and exorbitantly given to sensual pleasures, that wise people never employ him: as believing such men to be mere *good-for-nothings.* Because a wretched world will continue indisposed unto the Kingdom of the glorious and only Saviour, and say, of our *Immanuel,* "We will not have this man to reign over us"; it is therefore very much put over into the hands of such selfish, and sensual and wicked *rulers:* and very—*centaurs.* While the deserved *curse* of God remains upon an impious, and besotted world, there must be few *rulers* that will seriously and strenuously *devise good,* and seek to be *blessings* unto it. *Rulers* must, alas, how often be men, whose *lives* are not worth a *prayer,* nor their *deaths* worth a *tear*. *Athanasius* [1] has well answered the question, whence 'tis that such worthless and wicked men get into authority? He says, " 'Tis, δια το Ειναι τον λαον πονηρον. The people are wicked and must be punished with men after their own heart." Thus, when a *Phocas* [2] was made Emperor, a religious man complained unto Heaven, *Cur fecisti eum Imperatorem?* Heaven gave to the complaint that answer, *Non inveni pejorem.*¶ Evil rulers are well reckoned by the historian, among the effects *divinae ultionis;* * they may go into the catalogue with *sword,* and *plague,* and *fire.* One man may be worse than all three. Such bring up the rear, in the train of the *pale horse:* [3] *the beasts of the earth.*

O our God, our God, when will thy compassions to a miserable world, appear in bestowing upon it good rulers, able men, such as fear God, men of truth, hating covetousness? Oh! that the time were come, when there shall be a ruler over men, the Just One, thy JESUS, *ruling in the fear of God, and He shall be as the light of the morning, when the sun riseth; and under Him, the mountains shall bring peace to the people, and the little hills by righteousness; and He will according to His Word make our officers peace, and our exactors righteousness. Hasten it, in thy time, O Lord; but, how long, O Lord, holy and true, dost thou not judge! And make the kingdoms of this world, thy own, and remove them that corrupt the earth; and in a great chain bind up him, who pretends that the kingdoms of the world are his, and those who are the rulers of the darkness of this world!*

O all you that love God, add your *Amen,* to *hasten the coming of this day of God!*

In the meantime:

It cannot be expressed, how much *good* may be done, by a

¶ Why did you elect him Emperor? . . . I could not find a worse [man].

* of divine judgment [punishment].

chief magistrate of a country, who will make the *doing of good*, his *chief intention*: a *Constantine*, or a *Theodosius*, or a *Gratian*.[4] The first of these, notwithstanding the vast cares of the Empire to take up his time, yet would every day at stated hours, retire into his closet and on his *knees* offer up his *prayers* unto the glorious GOD. But then, that he might recommend this duty unto the world; this admirable emperor caused his *image* in all his *gold coins*, and his *pictures* and *statues*, to be made in a *praying posture*, with his *hands* extended, and his *eyes* lifted up, to Heaven. O *imperial piety!* To behold such a prince at the head of it, one would think, were enough to *convert a world!* It would, if it were not for the dreadful energies of one, who is by the *wrath* of God become, *the Prince of this world!* I say,

The virtuous *example* of such an one, is almost enough to reform whole nations! It carries irresistible *charms* with it, by which *totus componitur orbis*.† A *prince* exemplary for piety, sheds the rays of Heaven, as the *sun shining* in his meridian *strength*, with a most penetrating force into the people, *rejoicing under his wings*. 'Tis now a rarity; but it will not be so, in the approaching age, when the *kings of the earth, shall bring their glory and honor* into the Holy City! A *little piety* in princes, makes a glaring show; the eyes of their subjects are dazzled, their minds ravished, with it: they *numinize* them. What would be done by a *degree* of *piety* in them, that should bear proportion to the *degree* of their *quality;* and if their *piety* were as much above that of other men, as their *station?* Roll about, O *age*, that shall bring on such admirable *spectacles!*

'Tis a vast influence that such might have on the *reformation* of the world, and by consequence on its *felicity*, by dispensing *preferments* and *employments* to none but such as may by virtue be recommended unto them.[5] If good men generally

† all the world is put in order.

were put into *commissions*, and none but good men made *commanders* at *sea*, and on *shore*, what a mighty *change for the better* would the world immediately be blessed withal! I will beg leave to say, It will be a most comprehensive service unto a nation, to get them unfettered from any *test*, that may render honest and faithful men, uncapable of serving them. And, I will take leave also to say: The *displacing of a few officers* on the score of their being found *vicious men*, would signify an hundred times as much to mend the state of a depraved, betrayed, unprosperous nation, as a thousand *proclamations against vice* followed with no such executions.

Good laws are important *machines*, to keep very much *evil* out of the world; yea, they reach none, without the *doing of some good* unto them. All that have any share in the *legislative power*, ought very much to be concerned, that such *good laws* may be enacted as may be for a lasting benefit. The *representatives* of a people, in their *Parliaments*, or *Assemblies*, will do well, to think, "What is there still defective in our laws, leaving the iniquities or necessities of men yet not provided against?" And, "What further laws may be propounded, that the reign of holiness and righteousness may be advanced?" There have been *laws* (and sometimes none of the best, but *mischiefs established by laws!*) which have made the *names* of those that first moved for them to be remembered. The remembrance of having been, *the man that first moved a good law*, were better than a statue erected for one's memory. But if other men forget it, Sirs, you will not want a recompense in God's, and your own remembrance of it. You know whose prayer it was, *Think upon me, my God, for good, according to all that I have done for this people!* [6]

Magistrates may do an unknown deal of good, by countenancing of worthy *ministers*. To *settle* and *support* such *men of God* in a place, is to be, as one may say, the *grandfathers* of all the *good* which those men shall do in the place. Their

95

consultations, and their *combinations*, with able, faithful, zealous *ministers*, may produce more good effects than ever any astrology foretold of the most happy *conjunction*. When *Moses* and *Aaron* [7] join to *do good*, what can't they do? Queen *Elizabeth* admired the happiness of *Suffolk*, in her progress, where she saw a mighty good understanding between virtuous *magistrates* and faithful *ministers*.

Briefly. We will observe a *decorum* in our PROPOSALS, and not suppose *unattentiveness* or *incapacity* in those to whom we offer them. It shall only be proposed, that since MAGISTRATES are usually *men of abilities*, they would retire sometimes to a contemplation on that generous point, *What good may I do in the world?* And observe, what they are *able themselves* (assisted by the implored grace of Heaven) to *find out*, as part of the *good*, which they are to do in *serving their generation*.

I forget myself, if old *Theognis* [8] had not a maxim, which must not be forgotten. "When the administration of affairs, is placed in the hands of men, proud of command, and bent to their own private gain, be sure the people will soon be a miserable people." I propose that the maxim should be remembered, and this mischief avoided.

And this one thing more, *Thinkest thou this, O man that judgest, that thou shalt escape the Judgment of God?* [9] Let the *judges* of the people, consider, that God will one day bring them into *judgment—Judex nuper eram; jam judicor.*‡ Oh, that *rulers* would *realize* to themselves, as *real* a matter as any in the world! That they must give an *account* unto God, concerning their administration of their *government*. Sirs, the great GOD, before whom the biggest of you all is but as a worm of the dust, will demand an account of you, *how faithful you were in the discharge of your office? What you did for His Kingdom in your office? Whether you did what you could, that the world might be the better for you?* If you would

‡ Until recently I was a judge; now I am judged.

often take this awful matter in your consideration, which, oh! what *reason* you have to do!—it could not but quicken you to very many actions, which would be *no grief of heart* unto you another day! He was one of the best *rulers*, that ever was in the world, whose thoughts run upon that point: "What shall I do when God rises up, and when He visits, what shall I answer Him?" Even *Abubeker* the successor of *Mahomet*, upon an expostulation with him for his walking on foot, when he took a view of his army, said, "I shall find my account with God for these steps." He has less Christianity than a *Mahometan*, who is utterly unmindful of *the account he must give to God, of the steps taken by him.*

How well did things go at *Neo-Caesarea*, when *Basil*,[10] who lived there, could give that account, concerning the Governor of the place! "That he was a most exact observer of *justice;* but very *courteous*, and *obliging*, and *easy of access* to the oppressed: he was equally at leisure for the *rich* and for the *poor;* but all *wicked people* were afraid of him: he abhorred exceedingly the taking of a *bribe:* and his design, in short, was to raise *Christianity* unto its pristine *dignity*." A *Mahometan* Captain General, whose name was *Caled*, said once unto a Christian: "It does not at all become men in eminent station, to deal deceitfully and use tricks." It is a miserable thing, when a *Christian* in *eminent station*, will do such things!

[CHAPTER EIGHT: PHYSICIANS]

§18. The PHYSICIAN (who sometimes comes also to be a *magistrate;* and *Aristotle* has a saying very contrary to the *Jewish* maxim, that *a city will be happy under such a government!*), he also has his opportunities to *do good*, and render himself, *a beloved physician*, which he is to be advised of.

Zaccuth the *Portuguese*,[1] who among many other books written by him, wrote *An History of the Principal Physicians*, was one, who after he had got into *Amsterdam*, did by *circumcision* render it evident, that he had until then, and for thirty years together, only *dissembled Christianity* at *Lisbon;* yet because he was very *charitable to poor patients*, he was very much esteemed. We now apply ourselves to those, whose *love* to Christianity, we hope, is *without dissimulation*. There is to be expected from them, a *charity* and an *usefulness*, which may entitle them to a remembrance in a better *history* than that of *Zacutus Lusitanus;* yea, in that *Book of Life*, where a name will be of more account, than to be found in the *Vitae Illustrium Medicorum*,§ where *Peter Castellanus*[2] has embalmed so many of that profession.

By serious and shining *piety* in your own *example*, you will bear a glorious testimony to the *cause of God and religion*. You will glorify the *God of Nature*, and the only Saviour. Your acquaintance with *Nature*, will indeed be your condemnation, if you do it not. Nothing so *unnatural* as to be *irreligious. Religio Medici*,‖[3] has the least reason of any under Heaven, to be an, *irreligion*. It has been most unreasonably done of them, who have administered occasion, and [justifi-

§ Lives of Well-known Physicians.
‖ The Religion of the Physician.

98

cation?] for that complaint of *Christians: Ubi tres medici, tres athei.*¶ It is very sad, that when we read about the state of the *Rephaim* [4] in the other world, the *physicians* are by so many translators (they think, with too much cause) carried into it. Very sad, that the *Jews* imagine they have had cause to say, *Optimus inter medicos ad Gehennam;* * and assign this cause for so severe a sentence: *Non enim metuit a morbis; vescitur laute, nec confringit cor suum Deo; aliquando etiam interficit homines, quando pauperes, quos posset, non sanat.*† A sad story, if it be true!

Sirs; you will never count yourselves to be such *adeptists*, as to be *at a stand* in your studies, and make no further progress in your inquiries, into *maladies*, and after *medicines*. A *physician come to his full growth*, looks dangerously and ominously. Had the world gone on, with nothing but an *Æsculapius*,[5] furnished with a *goat* (whose *milk* for *pharmacy*) and a *dog* (whose *tongue* for *chirurgery*),[6] we had been miserably of it. You will be diligent, and studious, and inquisitive; and still, *read* much, and *think* more, and *pray* most of all; and be solicitous, to *find out*, and *give out*, something very considerable for the *good of mankind*, which none before you has lit upon: be solicitous to make some addition to the treasures of your noble profession. Though to attain the honor of being a *Sydenham* [7]—*Non cuivis homini contingit;* ‡ however, *to do something*, may be a laudable ambition.

By the benefit they expect from you, and by the charms of your polite education and proper and prudent conversation, you are sometimes introduced into the *familiar acquaintance* of *great men*. Persons of the first quality entertain you, with

¶ Where there are three physicians, there are three atheists.

* The best among the physicians [will go] to hell.

† He is not afraid of sickness; he feeds himself lavishly, and he does not offer his heart to God; sometimes he even kills men, when he neglects the poor whom he might cure.

‡ does not happen to every man.

much freedom, and friendship, and familiarity. Perhaps, you become, under *Hippocrates's* Oath,[8] almost a sort of *confessors* unto them: as indeed, the *confessors* were usually the *physicians* of the people, for several ages. What an advantage to *do good*, have you in your hands, by this acquaintance? The poor *Jews* both in the *Eastern* and in the *Western* parts of the world, have many a time, had very *good offices* done for their nation, by means of their countrymen arriving to be *physicians in ordinary* unto the *princes* of the countries where they have been dispersed. Sirs, your admission to feel the pulse of *eminent persons*, may enable you, to do many *good offices* for many *good interests*. You are persons of that *acumen*, that you need not be told, *what!* You will soon discover excellent things and ways, wherein *good* may be done, if you will please to deliberate upon it: "What good motions may I make to my patient, that he may do good in the world?" If you read what *Gregory Nazianzen* writes of his brother *Caesarius*, a famous physician, and a man of honor, you will doubtless find your dispositions this way enkindled. You know, how ready the *sick* are, to hear *good motions;* and how seasonable it is to ply them therewith, when a begun *recovery* from sickness, bespeaks their gratitude unto the *God of their health*. Yea, and for them that are in health also, you may find, *mollissima tempora fandi.*§

Physicians often are *men universally learned*. They have *treasure* enough, and sometimes *leisure* enough, to write Books, on a vast variety of subjects, whereby *knowledge* and *virtue* may be greatly advanced in the world. The late *epic poems* of a *Blackmore,*[9] and *Cosmologia Sacra* of a *Grew,*[10] are fresh examples; mankind is indebted unto those learned physicians; the names of the *heroes* are immortalized; they need no *statues:* nor need they mind the envy of any modern *Theophrastus.*[11] A *catalogue* of Books written, on various arguments, besides

§ the best times for speaking [to advise them to do good].

PHYSICIANS

those of their own profession (and unto better purpose, too,
than only to produce *Erastianism* [12] in the churches which our
Glorious Lord has instituted), by *learned physicians*, would
itself alone almost make a *book*. In the *great army* of *learned
physicians*, that have *published* their labors about the *Word
which the Lord has given*, and for the service of His Church,
and world, I humbly move, that the incomparable *Zwinger*,
and *Gesner* [13] may appear as *field-officers*. A city *Tauris* [14] were
too mean a present, for *physicians* of such merits. I propose
them to imitation; that many may *follow such leaders*. You
know, *Freher* [15] has brought on his *theater*, near five hundred
famous *physicians*, with some account of their *lives* and *works;*
very few *Britons* among them; and none at all that lived unto
the end of the former century. What a vast addition might
there be since made unto that *list of honor* from the *British*
nations! May an excellent ambition to be part of it, excite the
capable, to *do worthily!*

Physicians are even overstocked with opportunities, to help
the *poor*, and heal them for nothing. It was a noble saying of
*Cicero, Nil habet Fortuna melius, quam ut possis, neque natura
Praestantius, quam ut velis, servare plures.*|| But I will set be-
fore you an higher consideration, than what a pagan *Kirker* [16]
was ever acquainted with. Sirs, the more charity, and compassion, and condescension you treat the *poor* withal, the more
will you arrive to, *the greatest of all glories:* I say, the *greatest*
and *highest* of all glories!—I mean, an imitation of your admirable SAVIOUR. You will readily say, *Quod decuit* CHRISTUM,
cur mihi turpe putem? ¶ In comparison of this consolation, it
will be a small thing to say unto you, that your coming among
the *poor*, will be like the descent of the angel of *Bethesda* [17]

|| Fortune can give you nothing better than the power, and Nature
nothing more excellent than the desire, to save [or serve] many people.
¶ Why do I consider shameful to me that which was worthy of
Christ?

unto them. We will not presume to prescribe unto you, what *good* you shall do to the *poor*, and by what generous actions you shall *take their infirmities and bear their sicknesses*. Only we enter an objection against your taking any *fees* for your *visits* on the *Lord's-Days;* because, the *time* is none of *yours;* 'tis the *Lord's!*

When we consider how much the *lives* of men are in the *hands* of God; and what a dependence we have on the *God of our health* for our cure, when we have lost it; and what strange and strong *proofs* we have had, of *angels* by their communications or operations contributing to the cure of the diseases wherewith *mortals* have been oppressed (whereof I can myself relate astonishing instances!); and the marvelous efficacy of *prayer* for the recovery of a *sick brother, who has not sinned a sin unto death;* what better thing is there to be recommended unto a *physician,* who desires to *do good,* than this: *Good Sir, be a man of prayer.* In your daily and secret *prayer* carry every one of your *patients* by name (as you would your own children) unto the glorious *Lord our Healer,* for His healing *mercies:* place them as far as your *prayer* will do it, under the *beams* of the *Sun of Righteousness.* And as any *new case* of your patients may occur, especially if there be any difficulty in it, why should you not make your particular and solicitous applications to Heaven for direction! *O Lord, I know that the way of man is not in himself, nor is it in man, that walketh, to direct his steps;* no, nor in man that healeth, to perform his cures. *Hippocrates* advised physicians, that when they visited their patients, they should consider, whether there might not be, *divinum quiddam in morbo.** Truly, in some sense, there is ever so, and it should be considered. What an *heavenly life* might you lead, if your business may be carried on with as many visits to *Heaven,* as you make unto your *patients!* One *Jacob Tzaphalon,* a famous Jew in the former

---

* something divine in sickness.

century, published at *Venice,* a book entitled *Precious Stones.* There are several *prayers* in the book; and among them a pretty long one, *for physicians when they go to visit their patients.* When the Psalmist says, "Thou hast made me wiser than my enemies"; it may be read, "Thou hast made me wise from my Enemies." We should learn *wisdom* from them; *fas est, et ab hoste!* †—O *Christianity,* certainly thou wilt outdo *Judaism* in thy devotions!

We read, "Heaviness in the heart of man makes it stoop, but a good word makes it glad." We read, "A cheerful heart doth good like a medicine, but a broken spirit drieth the bones." And *Baglivi* [18] is not the only physician, who has made the observation, "That a great part of our diseases, either do rise from, or are fed by, a *weight of cares* lying on the *minds* of men. Diseases that seem *incurable,* are easily cured by agreeable conversation. *Disorders* of the *mind,* first bring diseases on the *stomach;* and so the whole mass of blood gradually becomes infected. And as long as the *passions* of the *mind* continue, the *diseases* may indeed change their *forms,* but they rarely quit the patients." *Tranquillity of mind* will do strange things, towards the relief of *bodily maladies.* 'Tis not without reason, that *Hoffmann,*[19] in his dissertation, *Des Moyens de Vivre Longtemps,* does insist on *tranquillity of mind* as the chief among the *ways to live long;* and that this is the cause why we read, "The fear of the Lord tendeth to life." They that have practiced *the art of curing by expectation,* have made an experiment of what the *mind* will do towards the cure of the *body.* By practicing *the art of curing by consolation,* you may carry on the experiment. I propound then, let the *physician* with all possible ingenuity of *conversation,* find out, what matter of *anxiety,* there may have been upon the mind of his *patient;* what there is, that has made his life *uneasy* to him. Having discovered the *burden,* let him use all the ways he

† it is right, even from the enemy!

can devise to take it off. Offer him such *thoughts*, as may be the best *anodynes* for his distressed mind; especially, the *right thoughts of the righteous*, and the ways to a composure upon *religious principles*. Give him a *prospect*, if you can, of some *deliverance* from his distresses, or some *abatement* of them. Raise in him as *bright thoughts* as may be, and scatter the *clouds*, remove the *loads*, which his mind is perplexed withal: especially, by representing and magnifying the *mercy* of GOD in CHRIST unto him. It is possible, Sir, that you may in this way also, find our [out?] *obliging occasions* to exercise abundance of *goodness*, in doing yourself, or in bringing others to do, *kindnesses* for the miserable.

And what should hinder you, from considering the *souls* of your *patients*, their *interior state;* their *spiritual health;* what they *have done*, and what they *have to do*, that they may be in *good terms with Heaven?* You may from their *natural distempers*, affect your own minds, and theirs too, with a sense of our *analogous moral* ones. You may make your conversation with them, a *vehicle* for such *admonitions of piety* as may be most *needful* for them: that they may neither be found *unprepared* for *death*, nor *unthankful* and *unfruitful* upon their escaping of it. This you may do, without any indecent intrusion into the office of the *minister;* but you may indeed at the same time do many a good office for the *minister*, as well as for the *patient*, and inform the minister when and where and how he may be very serviceable among some of the miserable, with whose condition he may else happen to be unacquainted. The *art of healing* was, you know, first brought into order by men that had the *care of souls*. And I know not why they who profess and practice that noble *art*, should now wholly cast off that *care!* Perhaps you remember a *king*, who was also a *physician* (for other *crowned heads*, besides *Mithridates* and *Hadrianus* and *Constantinus Pogonatus*, have been so!) [20] and who gave this reason why the *Greeks* had such diseases among them so much uncured: *because they neglected their souls, the chief thing of all*. For my part, I know not why the *physician* should wholly *neglect the souls* of his patients!

I will hold you no longer. You are not ignorant, that *medicine* in the world, once was, and in many ungospellized parts of the world still is, *a thing horribly magical*. *Celsus* [21] tells it, as a part of the *Egyptian philosophy* current in his time, that the body of man is divided into *thirty-six* parts, each of which was the peculiar allotment and possession of a *demon;* and this *demon* was by the *Magi* called upon, to cure diseases of the part that belonged unto him. Even in *Galen's* time [22] we find *prestigiaturas Ægyptias* practiced; he himself writes of them. Other countries were from *Egypt* infected with them. Hence *medicines* were called, *pharmaca*.[23] The *Oriental* nations had their *Teraphim* for the cure of diseases. Whence θεραπευω signifies, both to *worship*, and to *cure*. And, *Curae Morborum*, is reckoned by *Eusebius* [24] one main article of the *pagan theology*. God used all proper means, for saving His people, from having to do with that sort of *men*, or of *means*. He commended unto them, the study of Nature, and of natural remedies. They did after the example of *Solomon*, study *botanics:* they had their *apothecaries* who were to furnish them with *materials* for medicines. The Princes of *Judea* had, as *Pliny* tells us, their *physic gardens*. Probably *Naboth's* vineyard [25] might have such an one in it; which might be the reason why *Ahab* did so covet it. And *Joram*, the son of *Ahab*, repaired hither, to be cured of his wounds.[26] An excellent physician, in a late composition with which he has obliged the public, thinks the sin of *Asa*,[27] when he *sought not unto the Lord, but unto the physicians*, was both occasioned and aggravated by this: there were at this time none but *magical physicians*. But some others have thought, that some of *Asa's* ancestors had been *medically* disposed, and were students in the *art of healing*. From hence might come the name of *Asa:* for *Asa* is the *Chaldee* word for a *physician.* It may be, for that cause this king might have the greater esteem for those who were skilled in *medicines,* and put a *confidence* in them, that had with it and in it, a neglect of the glorious GOD; the only Author and Giver of health. What I aim at, in this paragraph, is but summarily to bespeak the *reverse* of all this; that my honorable *Asa* (*honorable!* the son of *Sirach* has taught me to call him so!) would himself continually go to *God our Saviour* on all occasions, and as far as he can, bring all his *patients* thither also.

Finally: an industrious and an ingenious gentleman of your profession, has a passage in a preface to his *Pharmacopaeia Bateana,*[28] which I will here insert; because very many of you can speak the like; and by inserting it, I propose, to increase the number.

"I know no poor creature that ever came to me in my whole time, that once went from me, without my desired help *gratis.* And I have accounted the restoration of such a poor and wretched creature, a greater blessing to me, than if I had gotten the wealth of both the *Indies.* I can't so well express myself concerning this matter, as I can conceive it; but I am sure, I should have been more pleased, and had a greater satisfaction, in seeing such an helpless creature restored to its desired health, than if I had found a very valuable treasure. All the good I have done in these cases, as I never can repent it, so I resolve to continue it; for I certainly know, I have had the signal blessing of God, attending my endeavors, for it."

[CHAPTER NINE: RICH MEN]

§19. *I will get me unto the rich men,—and will speak unto them:* for they will *know the ways* to *do good*, and will think, what they shall be able to say, when they come into the *Judgment of their God*. An English person of quality, quoting that passage, "The desire of a man is his kindness," invited me so to read it, "The *only* desirable thing in a man is his goodness." How happy would the world be if every person of quality would come into this persuasion! It is an article in my commission: "Charge them that are rich in this world, that they do good, that they be rich in good works, ready to distribute, willing to communicate." In pursuance thereof, I will put *rich men* in mind of the opportunities to *do good*, with which the God, who *gives power to get wealth*, has favored and obliged and enriched them. It was an account, and a very good one it was, that has been sometimes given of a good man: "The wealth of this world, he knew no good in it, but the doing of good with it." Yea, those men who have had very little *goodness* in them, yet in describing *the manners of the age*, in which they have had perhaps themselves too deep a share, have seen cause to subscribe and publish this prime dictate of reason: "We are never the better for anything, barely for the propriety's sake; but it is the application of it, that gives everything its value. Whoever buries his talent, breaks a sacred trust, and cozens those that stand in need on't." Sirs, you cannot but acknowledge, that it is the Sovereign GOD, who has bestowed upon you, the *riches* which distinguish you. A *devil* himself, when he saw a *rich man*, could not but make this acknowledgment unto the God of Heaven, "Thou hast blessed the work of his hands, and his substance is increased in the land." It is also a thing, whereof 'tis to be hoped, you are not unapprehensive, that the *riches* in your possession are some of the *talents*, whereof you must give an account unto the glorious LORD, who has betrusted you therewithal: and that you will *give up your account with grief, and not with joy,* if it must be found, that *all* your estates have been laid out, only to gratify the appetites of the *flesh,* and *little* or *nothing* of them consecrated unto the service of *God,* and of His Kingdom in the world. We read of the servants assigned unto the *priests* of old, "Unto you they are given as a gift for the Lord." It is what is to be said of all our *estates.* What God gives us, is not given us for ourselves, but *for the Lord.* And, *cum crescunt dona crescunt etiam rationes donorum.‡* Indeed there is hardly any professor of Christianity, so *vicious,* but he will own, that all of his estate is to be used in *honest uses;* and part of it, in *pious uses.* If any plead their *poverty,* to excuse them, and exempt them, from doing anything this way, O *poor widow* with thy *two mites,* eternized in the history of the Gospel,[1] thou shalt *rise up in the Judgment with that generation, and shalt condemn them.* And let them also know, that they take a course, to condemn and confine themselves unto eternal *poverty.* But the main question is, about the *quota parts;* how much of a man's income is to be devoted unto *pious uses?* And now, let it not seem an *hard saying,* if I say unto you, that a *tenth part* is the least that you can bring under a more *solemn dedication* unto the Lord; for whom indeed, after some sort, we are to lay out our *all.* A farthing less, would make an enlightened and considerate Christian, suspicious, of his coming under the danger of a *sacrilege.* By the *pious uses* for which your *tenths* are thus challenged, I do not intend only the *maintenance of the evangelical ministry,* but also the relief of the *miserable* whom our merciful Saviour has made the receivers of His rents, and all that is to be more directly done, for the preserving and pro-

‡ as the gifts increase, so also increase the reasons for [giving] gifts.

moting of *piety* in the world. Since there is a *part* of every man's revenues due to the glorious Lord, and such *pious uses,* it is not fit that the determination of *what part,* it must be, should be left unto such hearts as ours. My friend, thou hast, it may be, too high an opinion of thy own *wisdom* and *goodness,* if nothing but thy own *carnal heart,* shall determine still *when,* and *what,* thy revenues are to do, for Him, whom thou art so ready to *forget,* when He has *filled* thee. But if the LORD Himself, to whom thou art but a *steward,* has fixed any *part* of our usual *revenues,* for Himself, as 'tis most reasonable that He should have the fixing of it, certainly a *tenth* will be found the least that He has called for. A *tenth* is the *least part* in the first division of numbers, which is that of *unites. Grotius* notes it, as the foundation for the law of tithes: *Numerus denarius gentibus ferme cunctis numerandi finis est.*§ It is but fair, and the very *light of Nature* will declare for it; that the great GOD, who with a *seventh day,* is owned as the *Creator,* should with a *tenth part* be owned as the *possessor* of all things. We don't allow Him so much as *the least,* if we withhold a *tenth* from Him. Less than *that,* is less than what all nations make *the least.* Certainly, to withhold this, is to *withhold more than is meet.* Sirs, you know the *tendency.* Long before the *Mosaic* dispensation of the Law, we find, that this was *Jacob's* vow: "The Lord shall be my God, and of all that Thou shalt give me, I will surely give the tenth unto Thee." [2] It seems we do not sufficiently declare, *that the Lord is our God,* if we do not *give a tenth* unto Him. And how can we approve ourselves *Israelites indeed,* if we sleight such a pattern of our *Father Jacob?* I will ascend a little higher. In one text we read of our *Father Abraham,* "He gave Melchizedek the tenth of all." [3] In another text we read of our Saviour JESUS, "Thou art a priest forever after the Order of Melchizedek." [4] Hence I form this argument: the rights of *Melchizedek* belong to our

§ Nearly all people reckon that a tenth part is the limit.

JESUS, the *Royal High-Priest* now concerned in the Heavens for us. The *tenths* were the right of *Melchizedek.* Therefore the *tenths* belong to our JESUS. I do in my conscience believe, *that this argument cannot be answered.* The man seems to blur one evidence of his being one of the true children of *Abraham,* that goes to answer it. I do renew my *appeal* to the *light of Nature. To nature thou shalt go!* 'Tis very certain, that the ancient pagans did use to *decimate* for *sacred uses. Pliny* tells us, the *Arabians* did so. *Xenophon* tells us, the *Grecians* did so. You find the custom, as old as the pen of *Herodotus* can carry it. 'Tis confirmed by *Pausanias,* and by *Diodorus Siculus.* A whole army of authors, besides *Doughty,* have related this, and asserted it. I will only bring in *Festus,* to speak for them all: *Decima quaeque veteres dijs suis offerebant.*|| *Christian,* wilt thou do less for thy GOD, than the poor perishing *pagans* did for theirs? [5] *Oh! tell it not!*—But this I will tell: that they who have conscientiously employed their *tenths* in *pious uses,* have usually been blessed in their estates, with a very remarkable Providence of God. The blessing has been sometimes delayed, with some trial of their *patience: not for any injustice in their hands;* their *prayer* has been *pure.* And their *faith* of the *future state* has been sometimes tried, by their meeting with some losses, and some disappointments. But then, their *little* has been so blessed, as to be still a *competency;* and God has blessed them with so much *contentation* in it, that it has yielded *more* unto them, than the *much* of many others. And *very often,* I say, *very often,* they have been rewarded with a strange success, and increase of their estates; even in this world, seen the fulfilment of that Word: "Cast thy grain into the moist ground; for thou shalt find it after many days." [6] And that word: "Honor the Lord with thy substance; so shall thy barns be filled with plenty." [7] History has given us many and charming examples, of those, who have had their conscientious

|| What the ancients offered their gods were tithes.

decimations followed and rewarded with a surprising prosperity of their affairs; and small *mechanics*, or *husbandmen*, have risen to estates, which once they never durst have dreamed of. The excellent *Gouge*, in his treatise entitled *The Surest and Safest Way of Thriving*,[8] has collected some such examples. The Jewish proverb, *Decima, ut Dives fias*; or, *Tithe and be rich!* would be oftener verified, if oftener practiced. *Prove me now herewith, saith the Lord of Hosts, if I will not pour out a blessing upon you!* [9] But let the demand of *liberal things* grow upon you. *A tenth,* I have called, *the least.* For some, 'tis much *too little.* Men of great estates, that would not *sow for their flesh, and reap corruption,* may and will often go beyond a *decimation.* Some of them rise to a *fifth;* and the religious Countess of *Warwick*,[10] would not stop at any thing short of a *third.* The gentlemen my readers, will excuse me, if I carry them no higher, and say nothing to them, of a *Joannes Eleemosynarius*,[11] who annually made a distribution of all to pious uses; and having made even with his revenues, then said, "I bless God that I have now nothing left, but my Lord and Master Christ, whom I long to be withal, and whom I can with unentangled wings now fly unto!" Yet I will mention to them the example of some eminent merchants, who have set their estates at a moderate and competent elevation, and resolved, they would never be any *richer* than *that.* They have carried on a great and quick trade; but whatever *gain* carried their estates beyond the *set sum*, they devoted it all to *pious uses.* And were any of them, ever *losers?* Never one of them! The Christian Emperor *Tiberius* II [12] was *famous* for his religious bounties; his Empress thought him even *profuse*, in them. He told her, *he should never want money so long as in obedience to the command of a glorious Christ, he did supply the necessities of the poor, and abound in such religious bounties.* Once, immediately after he had made a liberal distribution, he unexpectedly found a mighty treasure; and there were tidings also brought him, of the death of a man vastly rich, who had bequeathed all his wealth unto him. Lesser men can tell very many, and very taking stories of this importance, even from their own happy experience. I cannot forbear transcribing some lines of my honored *Gouge* on this occasion.

"I am verily persuaded, that there is seldom any man, who giveth to the poor proportionably to what God has bestowed on him, but if he does observe the passages of God's Providence towards him, he shall find the same doubled and redoubled upon him in *temporal blessings*. I dare challenge all the world, to give one instance (or at least any considerable number of instances) of any *merciful man*, whose charity has undone him. But, as *living wells*, the more they are drawn, the more freely they spring and flow; so the substance of charitable men, does oftentimes multiply in the very distribution; even as the five loaves and few fishes did multiply in their breaking and distributing; and the widow's oil increased by the pouring it out."

I will add a consideration, wherein, methinks, common *humanity* should be sensible of a *provocation*. Let *rich* men who are not *rich towards God*, especially such as have no children of their own, to make the *heirs* of their *hoarded riches*, consider the vile ingratitude, which the *forks* that come after them, will treat them, withal. Sirs, they will hardly allow you a *tombstone;* and, wallowing in the *wealth* which you have left (but they complain, that you left it *no sooner* unto them), they will only play upon your *memory*, squib upon your *husbandry*, ridicule all your *parsimony!* How much more *wisdom*, would it be, for you to *do good* with your estates while you *live;* and at your *death* do *that*, which may embalm your name to posterity in this world, and be for your advantage in that which you are going unto! That your *souls* may *dwell* in all the *ease* and *good* of the *Paradisian* reflections, at the time, when others *inherit* what you leave unto them.

I only now annex the compliment of one to his friend, upon his accession to an estate: "Much good may it do you; that is, much good may you do with it."

I hope, we are now ready for PROPOSALS. We shall set ourselves, *to devise liberal things.*

Gentlemen, it is of old said, *res est sacra miser.*¶ To *relieve the necessities of the poor (non pavistis, occidistis);* * this is a thing acceptable to the compassionate God; who has given to *you,* what He might have given to *them;* and has given it unto *you* that you might have the *honor* and *pleasure* to impart it unto *them:* and who has told you, *He that has pity on the poor, lends unto the Lord.*[13] The more you consider the *command* and *image* of a glorious CHRIST in what you do this way, the more assurance you have, that in the *day of God,* you shall joyfully hear Him saying, *You have done it unto me!* And the more humble, silent, reserved *modesty* you express, concealing even from the *left hand* what is done with the *right,* the more you are assured of, *a great reward in the heavenly world.* Such *liberal* men, 'tis observed, are usually *long-lived* men. *Fructus liberat arborem.*† And at last, they pass from this unto *everlasting life.*

The name of a LADY, what is it in the original sense of the word? It was first, *leafdian,* then *lafdy:* from *leaf,* or *laf,* which signifies, *a loaf of bread.* And from *d'ian* to *serve.* As much as to say, *one who distributes bread.* The true LADY, is one who feeds the *poor,* and makes agreeable *distributions* to their *indigencies.* In the days of primitive Christianity, the *ladies* of the best quality, would seek and find out the *sick,* and visit the *hospitals,* and see what help they wanted; and help them with an admirable alacrity. The mother, and the sister of *Nazianzen,* what a *good report* have they obtained from his pen, for their

¶ A poor man is sacred.

* not to crush them or to ruin them.
† Gathering the fruit relieves the tree.

unwearied bounties to the *poor?* Empresses themselves have stooped, and they never looked so *great,* as in their stooping, to relieve the miserable:

> . . . *And when they stoop'd, it was to do*
> *Some good to others. Angels, they do so!*

When you keep your *days* of *prayers,* now is a special season for your *alms:* that your *prayers* may go up with your *alms,* as a *memorial before the Lord.* Verily, there are *prayers* in *alms.* And, *Is not this the fast that I have chosen, saith the Lord;* [14] the note of the beggar among the Jews was, *Deserve something by me.* Among us, it may be, *Obtain something by me.*

There is a city in the world, where every house hath a box hanging in a chain, on which is written, *Think on the poor;* and they commonly conclude no bargain, but more or less is put into the box. The *deacons* have the key, and once a quarter go round the city, and take out the money. When that city was like to have been lost, one who was not the best man in the world, yet could say, *that he was of opinion, God would preserve that city from being destroyed, if it were only for the great charity they express to the poor.* 'Tis the richest city of the richest country, for its bigness, that ever was in the world. A city that it is thought, spends yearly in charitable uses, more than all the revenues which the whole fine country of the Grand Duke of *Tuscany* brings in to the arbitrary master of it. You know, *Manus pauperum est Christi Gazophylacium.*‡

When you dispense your *alms,* unto the *poor,* who know, what it is to *pray,* you may oblige them to *pray* for you by name every day. 'Tis an excellent thing to have, *the blessing of them that have been ready to perish, thus coming upon you.* Behold, a surprising sense in which you may be *praying al-*

‡ The poor man's hand is Christ's treasure-chest.

RICH MEN

ways. You are so, even while you are *sleeping,* if those whom you have so obliged are thus *praying* for you! And now, look for the accomplishment of that word: *Blessed* is he that considers the *poor; the Lord will preserve him and keep him alive; and he shall be blessed on the earth.*[15]

Very often your *alms* are dispersed among such as very much need *admonitions of piety* to accompany them. Can't you contrive, to intermix a *spiritual charity,* with your *temporal?* Perhaps you may discourse with them about the *state of their souls,* and obtain from them, which you now have a singular advantage to do, some *declared resolutions* to do what they ought to do. Or else you may convey little *books* unto them, which certainly they will promise to *read,* when you thus bespeak their doing so.

Charity to the *souls* of men, is undoubtedly the highest and the noblest *charity,* and of the greatest consequence. To furnish the poor with *Catechisms,* and *Bibles,* is to do an unknown deal of *good* unto them: To publish and scatter *books of piety,* and to put into the hands of mankind such *treatises of divinity* as may have a tendency to make them *wiser* or *better;* no man knows what *good* he does in doing such things! It was excellently done of some good men, who, a little while ago were at the charge of printing thirty thousand of the *Alarm to the Unconverted,* written by Joseph Allein,[16] to be all given away unto such as would promise to read it. A man of no great estate [17] has before now with no great trouble, given away the best part of a thousand books *of piety,* every year for many years together. Who can tell, but with the expense of less than a shilling, Sir, you may *convert a sinner from the error of his way, and save a soul from death!* A worse doom, than a *damnatio ad metalla,*§ is upon the *soul,* who had rather hoard up his money, than employ it on such a *charity.*

He that *supports the office* of the *evangelical ministry,* sup-

§ condemnation to [work in] the mines.

115

ports a *good work;* and performs one; yea, at the second hand performs what is done by the skillful, faithful, painful minister, and that is *many* an one. The encouraged servant of the Lord, will do the more *good,* for your assistances, [if?] 'tis done for a glorious CHRIST, what you have done for *him;* and in consideration of the *glorious Gospel* preached by him. And you shall *receive a prophet's reward! Luther* said, *Si quid scholasticis confers, Deo ipsi contulisti.*‖ 'Tis more sensibly so, when the *scholars* are become godly and useful *preachers.*

I have read this passage: "It was for several years, the practice of a worthy gentleman, in renewing his leases, instead of making it a condition, that his tenants should keep an *hawk* or a *dog* for him, to oblige them, that they should keep a *Bible* in their houses, for themselves, and should bring up their children to *read* and be *catechized.*" *Landlords,* 'tis worth your considering, whether you may not in your *leases,* insert some *clauses,* that may serve the Kingdom of God. You are his *tenants,* in those very *freeholds,* where you are *landlords* to other men! Oblige your *tenants* to worship God in their families.

To take a *poor child,* especially an *orphan,* left in *poverty,* and bestow an *education* upon it, especially if it be a *liberal education,* is an admirable, and a complicated *charity;* yea, it may draw on a long train of *good,* and interest you in all the *good* that shall be done by those whom you have educated.

Hence also what is done for *schools,* and for *colleges,* and for *hospitals,* is done for a *general good.* The *endowing* of these, or the *maintaining* of them, is, *at once to do good unto many.*

But, alas, how much of the *silver* and *gold* in the world, is buried in hands, where 'tis little better than conveyed back to the *mines* from whence it came? Or employed unto as little purpose, as what arrives at "*Hindustan,*" where a large part of

‖ What you give to scholars you give to God himself.

the *silver* and *gold* of the world, is after a circulation carried as unto a fatal center, and by the *moguls* lodged in subterraneous caves, never to see the light any more. *Talia non facit bonae fidei ac spei Christianus.*¶

Sometimes there may be got ready for the press, elaborate composures, of great *bulk*, and greater *worth*, by which the best interests of *knowledge* and *virtue*, may be considerably served in the world [18] (perhaps, what may be called, as the *Octapla* [19] of *Origen* was, *opus ecclesiae*): they lie like the impotent man at the pool of *Bethesda;* and there they are like to lie, till God inspire some wealthy persons, to subscribe nobly for their publication, and by this generous application of their wealth to bring them abroad. The *names* of such noble benefactors to mankind, ought to *live*, as long as the *works* themselves; where the *works* do any good, what these have done towards the publishing of them, *ought to be told for a memorial of them.*

Yea, I will carry the matter further than so. The saying may seem to carry some affront in it: *Idle gentlemen and idle beggars, are the pests of the commonwealth.* But they that are offended must quarrel with the ashes of a Bishop. 'Twas Dr. *Sanderson's.* [20] Will you then think, Sirs, of some honorable and agreeable employments? I will mention one. The *Pythagoreans* forbade men's eating their own brains; or keeping their good thoughts to themselves. 'Tis an observation of the incomparable *Boyle,* "That as to *religious books* in general, it has been observed, that those penned by *laymen,* and especially *gentlemen,* have (*caeteris paribus*) * been better entertained, and more effectual than those of *ecclesiastics.*" We all know, his own were so. It is no rare thing for men of quality, to accomplish themselves in *languages* and *sciences,* until they have been prodigies of literature. Their *libraries* too, have been

¶ The Christian of good faith and hope does not do such things.

* other things being equal.

stupendous collections; approaching towards *Vatican* or *Bodleian* [21] dimensions. An *English gentleman* has been sometimes the most *accomplished thing in the whole world*. How many of these (besides a *Leigh*, a *Wolsely*, or a *Polhil*),[22] have been *benefactors* to mankind by their incomparable writings? It were mightily to be wished, that *rich men*, and persons of an elevated condition, would qualify themselves, for the use of the *pen*, as well as of the *sword;* and by their *pen* deserve to have it said of them, "They have written excellent things." An English *person of quality* in a book of his entitled, *A View of the Soul*,[23] has a passage, which I will address you with. Says he, "It is certainly, the highest dignity, if not the greatest happiness, human nature is capable of, here in the vale below, to have the soul so far enlightened as to become the mirror, or conduit, or conveyer of God's truth to others." It is an ill motto for men of capacity, MY UNDERSTANDING IS UNFRUITFUL. Gentlemen, consider what *subjects* may most properly and usefully fall under your *cultivation*. Your *pen* will stab *atheism* and *wickedness*, with an efficacy beyond other men's: If out of your *tribe* there come those who *handle the pen of the writer*, they will do uncommon execution. One of them has ingeniously told you: *Though I know some functions, yet I know no truths of religion, like the shewbread;* Matth. 12.4. only for the priests.

I will address you, with one PROPOSAL more. 'Tis, that you would (as *Ambrosius* [24] had his *Origen*), wisely choose a *friend* of shining abilities, of hearty affections, and of excellent piety: a *minister* of such a character, if it may be. And entreat him, yea, oblige him, to *study* for you, and *suggest* to you, *opportunities to do good:* make him, as I may say, your *monitor*. Let him advise you from time to time, what *good* you may do. Cause him to see, that he never gratifies you more, than by his advice upon this intention. If a *David* have a *seer* to do such a good office for him, and be on the *lookout* for to find out what good he may do, what services may be done for the *Temple* of God in the world!

There seems no need of adding anything but this. When *gentlemen* occasionally come together, why should not their *conversation* be agreeable to their superior quality? Methinks they should reckon it beneath people of their quality to employ their *conversation* with one another on trifling *impertinencies;* or at such a rate, that if their discourse were taken down in shorthand by one behind the hangings, they would blush to have it repeated unto them. *Nihil sed nugae, et risus, et verba proferuntur in ventum.*† Sirs, it becomes a *gentleman,* to entertain his company, with the finest *thoughts,* on the finest *themes!* But certainly, there cannot be any subject so worthy of a *gentleman* as this: *What Good there is to be Done in the World?* Were this noble subject oftener started in the conversation of *gentlemen,* an incredible deal of *good* would be done.

I will conclude with saying, you must *come forth* to any *public service* whereof you may be capable, when you are called unto it. Honest *Jeans* [25] has a pungent passage: "The World applauds the politic retiredness of those that bury their parts and gifts, in an obscure privacy, though both from God and man, they have a fair call to public employment; but the terrible censure of these men by Christ at the last Day, will discover them to be the arrantest fools, that ever were upon the face of the earth." That fault of not employing one's parts for the public, one calls, "a great sacrilege in the Temple of the God of Nature." It was a sad age, wherein *Tacitus* tells, *Inertia fuit sapientia.* ‡

† Nothing is said but trifles, laughter, words spoken to the wind.
‡ Inactivity was wisdom.

[CHAPTER TEN: OFFICIALS AND LAWYERS]

§20. You may remember, that one of the first of our PRO-POSALS was, for EVERYONE, to consider, *What is there that I may do for the service of God, and the welfare of man?* 'Tis to be expected, that all OFFICERS, *as such*, will conform, to what has been thus proposed. It should be the concern of all *officers*, from the *Emperor* to the *enomotarch*,[1] *to do all the good they can.* So then, there is the less need of making a more particular application to *lesser officers* of several sorts, who have *opportunities to do good*, more or less, in every one of their hands. However, they shall not all of them, complain that we have neglected them.

In the CHURCH, sometimes there are ELDERS (as in the primitive times, *Ecclesia seniores habuit*)§ who *rule well, though they labor not in the Word and doctrine.* It becomes these often to consider: "What shall I do, to prevent the rise of strife, or of any sin, that may be a root of bitterness in the flock? And, that Christ, and holiness may reign in it; and the Pastor have his ministry countenanced, encouraged, and prospered?" Their *visits* of the flock, and their endeavors to *prepare* people for *special ordinances*, may be of unknown advantage to religion.

There are DEACONS, entrusted with the *temporal affairs* of the society. It would be well, if these would oftener consider: "What may I do, that the Treasury of Christ may be increased?" And, "What may I do, that the life of my faithful pastor may be more comfortable to him!" And, "Whom of the flock do I think defective in their contributions to support the evangelical interests, and what shall I speak with great boldness in the Faith unto them?"

§ The church had its elders.

In the STATE, there are many officers, to whom the most significant and comprehensive PROPOSAL, that can be made, would be, *to consider their* OATHS. If they would seriously *ponder*, and faithfully *perform*, what their OATHS, oblige 'em to, a deal of *good* would be done.

But we must a little particularize.

The REPRESENTATIVES of any place: as they have opportunities to *do good* for the whole people, and should accordingly think, *what motions to make;* so they should be particularly solicitous for the *good* of that place, which has elected them.

Those whom we call, the SELECTMEN of a town, will fail a just expectation, if they do not inquisitively consider this point: "What shall I do, that I may be a blessing to the town, which I am now to serve?"

GRAND-JURYMEN, may very profitably consider: "What growing evils or nuisance, do I discover, whereof I shall do well to procure a presentation?" They should hold their *consultations*, upon this matter, as men in earnest for the *good* of the country.

Indeed, all *jurymen* should be, *boni homines*, that is to say, *good men*. Our old compellation of a neighbor, by the title, of, *Goodman*, was of this original; as much as to say, one qualified to *serve on a jury*. But then, let them *do good;* and contrive, how they may do it.

Why should CONSTABLES be excused! Their name (*constabularius*) first came, from the care of *making unruly horses to stand well together in the stable*. Sirs, 'tis very much *good* that you have to do, by being *masters of restraint*, in your walks, and otherwise, unto *unruly cattle*. What are vicious people (though perhaps *in honor*), but *like the beasts?* Well-disposed *constables* in a place, have done wondrous things, to keep up *good order* in it. Your thoughts on, "What good may I do?" and, your *consultations*, I beseech you!

And where TITHINGMEN are chosen and sworn, 'tis more

than a little *good,* which they may do, if they will conscientiously do their *duty.* Let them study well the *laws,* which lay down their *duty;* and let them also often consider, "What good may I do?" And consult with one another at certain times, to find out what they have to do, and assist and strengthen one another, in the doing of it.

I have done with the *civil list.*

MILITARY COMMANDERS have their opportunities to *do good.* They do it very much, when they uphold *exercises of piety,* in their several *regiments* and *companies.* And when they rebuke the *vices of the camp,* with a due severity. Might not *societies to suppress those vices,* be formed in the camp, to very good purpose, under their inspection? But if the *soldiers* ask, "What shall we do?," all my answer at present, is only: "Sirs, consider what you have to do."

COMMANDERS AT SEA, have their opportunities too. The more *absolute* they are in their command, the greater their opportunities. The *worship of God* seriously and constantly maintained aboard, will be of *good* consequence. A *body of good orders,* hung up in the steerage, and carefully executed, may prove that which all the people of the vessel may at last see cause to be very thankful for. *Books of piety* should also be taken aboard, and the men be called upon to retire for the perusal thereof, and for other pious actions.

But while our book seems to have so far discharged its office and purpose of *a counsellor,* as to leave no further expectations, there present themselves a considerable number of persons, who may justly complain of it, if among PROPOSALS to *do good,* they be left unconsidered. Some whom we do not find among them that addressed the blessed *morning-star* of our Saviour, for his direction, yet are now found among those who inquire, "And what shall we do?" [These are] The gentlemen of the LAW, who have that in their hands, the end whereof is, *to do good;* and the perversion of which from its professed end, is one of the *worst of evils.*

Gentlemen, your opportunities to *do good*, are such, and so liberal, and gentlemanly, is your education (for even for the common pleaders at the bar, I hope, that maxim of the law will not be forgotten: *Dignitas advocatorum non patitur ut in eam recipiatur, qui antea fuerat vilioris conditionis*): ‖ that PROPOS-ALS of what you *may do*, cannot but promise themselves an obliging reception with you. 'Tis not come to so sad a pass, that an *honest lawyer*, may as of old, the *honest publican*, require a statue, merely on the score of *rarity*. You may, if you study it, come to do so, on the score of universal and merito-rious *usefulness.*

In order to your being *useful*, Sirs, 'tis necessary that you be *skillful*. And that you may arrive to an excellent *skill in the law*, you will be well advised, what *authors* to study; *with the well-advised* in this point, there may be more than a little *wis-dom.* The knowledge of your own *statute-law*, is incontestably needful; and so, of the *common law*, which continually must accompany the execution of it. Here (besides needful *diction-aries*) you have your *Cokes*, and your *Vaughans*, and your *Wingates*, and your *Daltons*, and your *Kebles;* [2] and as many more, as you have time to converse withal. I am sorry to find a gentleman about the middle of the former century complain-ing about the *English law*, that the *books of it cannot be read over, under three or four years, with any deliberation; and that at an ordinary rate they cost above twenty pounds.* I do not propound so long and hard a task. For the *civil law* must also be known by them that would be well acquainted with *legal proceedings.* Volumes, huge ones and cartloads of them, have been written upon it; but among all these, methinks at least

‖ The dignity of lawyers does not permit a man of mean [or con-temptible] condition [or origin] to be admitted to the bar.

those two little ones, the *Enchiridion* of *Corvinus*, and *Arthur Duck's* treatise, *De Usu et Authoritate Juris Civilis*,¶ ought to be consulted, yea, digested, by one that would not be an *ignoramus*. I will be yet a little more free, in declaring my opinion. Had I learning enough to manage a cause of that nature, I should be very ready to maintain it at any *bar* in the world, that there never was known under the cope of Heaven, a more learned man, than the incomparable ALSTEDIUS.[3] He has written on every one of the subjects in the whole *circle of learning*, as accurately and as exquisitely as those men, who have spent all their lives in cultivating but any one of the subjects. The only reason, why his composures are no more esteemed, is, the *pleonasm* of his worth, and their deserving so much esteem. To hear some silly and flashy men, with a scornful sneer talk as if they had sufficiently done his business, by a foolish pun of *all's tedious*, is to see the ungrateful and exalted folly of the world; for *conciseness* is one of his peculiar excellencies; they might more justly call him anything than *tedious*. This digression only serves to introduce a recommendation of this excellent man's *Jurisprudentia*, as one of the best things a *lawyer* can be acquainted withal. I shall wrong it, if I say, *'Tis much in a little*; I must say, *'Tis all at once*.

A *lawyer* should be a *scholar*. It vexes one, that the Emperor *Justinian*, whose name is now upon the *laws* of the Roman Empire (because 'twas by his order *Tribonian* made his *hasty*, and some say *fallacious* and *unfaithful* collection of them, from the two thousand volumes, into which they had been growing for above a thousand years), is by *Suidas* [4] called Ἀναλφαβητος, *one that scarce knew his alphabet*. It is a vexation to find *Accursius*, one of the first glossators on the *laws*, fall into so many gross mistakes, through his ignorance; and unable to afford, when a sentence of Greek occurs in the text, any better gloss than this: *Haec Graica sunt, quae nec legi, nec intelligi*

¶ Of the Use and Authority of the Civil Law.

*possunt.** Though the thing were a trifle, it was no honor unto those writers on the *Pandect*, that they knew not what gender the name was of. It is odd, that when one title of the *law* is, *Of the signification of words*, the great interpreter of it, should leave it as a maxim, *De verbebus non curat juris consultus.*† However, a *Bartolus* has not so roughened your study, as a *Budaeas* has polished it.[5]

But, Sirs, when you are called upon to be *wise*, the main intention is, *that you may be wise to do good*. Without a disposition for this, *Doth not their excellency which is in them go away? They die even without wisdom.*[6] A foundation of *piety* must be first laid; an inviolable respect unto the *holy and just and good laws* of the infinite GOD. This must be the rule of all your actions; and it must particularly regulate your *practice of the law*. You are sensible, that it was ever the style of the *Civil Law*, to begin, *A Deo optimo maximo.*‡ Nor was it unusual for the instruments of the law, to begin with XP, the two first letters, abbreviating the name of ΧΡΙΣΤΟΣ § for which the notaries have ignorantly substituted an (X.P.) of later times. The life of the *lawyer* should have its beginning there, and be carried on with an eye thither. The Old *Saxon* laws had the TEN great precepts of the *Decalogue* prefixed in the front of them: *ten words*, in *two tables* of infinitely more account than the famous *twelve tables*, that were so admired by *Tully*, and by other antiquity; in the fragments whereof collected by your *Baldwin* and others, there are yet some things horribly unrighteous and barbarous.[7] These are to be the *first laws* with you: and as all the *laws* that are contrary to these, are *ipso facto* null and void, so in the *practice of the law*, everything that is disallowed by these, is to be avoided. The man whom the Scripture calls, *a lawyer*, was a *Karaite*, or one

* These are Greek things, which can neither be read nor understood.
† The jurisconsult does not worry about mere words.
‡ From the highest and greatest God.
§ Christ.

BONIFACIUS

who kept close to the *written Law* of God, in opposition to the *Pharisee,* and the *traditionist.* I know not why every *lawyer* should not still be in the best sense, a *Karaite.* By expressing a *reverence for the divine Law,* both that of *reason,* and that of superadded *Gospel,* you will *do good* in the world, beyond what you can imagine. You will redeem your honorable profession from the wrong which *ill men* have done to the reputation of it, and you will obtain another patronage for it, than what the satyr in the idle story of your Saint *Evona* has assigned it.[8]

Your celebrated *Ulpian* [9] wrote seven books, to show the several *punishments,* which ought to be inflicted on *Christians.* It is to be hoped, that you will invent as many *services* to be done unto the *cause of Christianity;* services to be done for the Kingdom of your Saviour; and methods to demonstrate your own being among the *best of Christians.*

I am not sure, our *Tertullian* was the gentleman of that name, who hath some *Consulta* in the Roman *Digesta:* some writers of his life (as well as *Grotius*) will not have it so. Yet *Eusebius* tells us, he was well skilled in the *Roman laws.* And in his writings you have many *law-terms;* particularly, *prescriptions* (the title of his treatises against *heretics*) were, as we learn from *Quintilian* and others, the *replies* of *defendants,* to the actions of the *plaintiffs.* I propose, that others of the faculty, study all possible *prescriptions* against them, who would hurt Christianity, and *apologies* for the Church and cause of our Saviour. But, Sirs, it must first of all be done, in your own virtuous, exact, upright conduct, under all temptations.

The miscarriages of some individuals, must not bring a blemish, on a noble and useful profession.

But many will be ready enough, to allow of a censure occurring in a late book entitled, *Examen Miscellaneum* (and I know scarce anything else worth quoting from it): "A lawyer that is a knave, deserves death, more than a band of robbers; for he

126

profanes the sanctuary of the distressed, and betrays the liberties of the people." To ward off such a censure, a *lawyer* must shun all those *indirect ways* of *making haste to be rich*, in which a man cannot be *innocent:* such as provoked the father of Sir *Matthew Hale*,[10] to give over the *practice of the law*, because of the extreme difficulty to preserve a *good conscience* in it. Sir, be prevailed withal, to keep constantly a *court of chancery* in your own breast; and scorn and fear to do anything, but what your *conscience* will pronounce, consistent with, yea, conducing to, *glory to God in the highest, on earth peace, good will towards men*. The very nature of your business, leads you to meditations on a *Judgment to come*. Oh! that you would so realize and antedate that *Judgment*, as to do nothing, but what you may verily believe, will be approved in it!

This piety must operate very particularly, in the *pleading of causes*. You will abhor, Sir, to appear in a *dirty cause*. If you discern, that your *client* has an *unjust cause*, you will faithfully advise him of it. *Utrum fallaciis et deceptionibus ad convincendum adversarium uti liceat?* ‖ This is the question. 'Tis to be hoped, that you have determined it like an *honest man*. You will be sincerely desirous, *Truth* and *Right* may take place. You will speak nothing that shall be to the prejudice of *either*. You will abominate the use of all unfair arts, to confound *evidences*, to browbeat *testimonies*, to suppress what may give light in the case. You have nothing against that old rule of pleading a cause: *Cognita iniquitate, a suscepto ejus patrocinio advocatus desistere debet.*¶

I remember *Schusterus*, a famous *lawyer* and *counsellor*, who died at *Heidelberg*, A.C. 1672, had one admirable stroke in his epitaph:

‖ Is it right to use deception in order to convince the adversary?
¶ The iniquity [or guilt of his client?] being known, the attorney must give up the case.

BONIFACIUS

Morti proximus vocem emisit;
Nihil se unquam suasisse consilio,
*Cujus jam jam moriturum peniteret.**

A *lawyer* who can go out of the world with such expressions, were a greater blessing to the world, than can be expressed.

I cannot encourage any gentleman, to spend much time in the study of the *Canon Law*: which *Baptista à Sancto Blasio*,[11] finds to contradict the *Civil Law* in two hundred instances. The *decrees*, and the *decretals*, and the *clementines* and *extravagants*, which compose the hideous volumes of that *law*, would compel any wise man, to make the apology, that one such made, for his aversion thereunto: *Non possum, Domine, vesci stercore humano.† Agrippa*,[12] who was a *doctor* thereof, said of that *law*, " 'Tis neither of God, nor for Him; nothing but corruption invented it; nothing but avarice has practiced it." *Luther* began the *Reformation* with burning of it. Nevertheless, there is one point in the *Canon Law* much insisted on, which well deserves very much of your consideration; that is, *restitution*. When men *get riches and not by right*, or have heaped up wealth in any *dishonest* and *criminal* ways, a *restitution* will be a necessary and essential ingredient of that *repentance*, which alone will find acceptance with Heaven. The awe of this thought may stand like an *angel with a drawn sword* in your way, when you may be under temptation to go out of your way after the *wages of unrighteousness*. Our *law* was once given unto us in *French*. Many of you, gentlemen, ken the *modern French* as well as the *ancient*. Monsieur *Placette* [13] has given you a valuable treatise, of RESTITUTION. In his treatise, there is a chapter, *Des cas où les Avocats sont obligés à*

---

* He who is about to die says: when he was dying he did not have to repent for any of the counsel he had ever given.

† I cannot feed myself, Lord, with human dung [or, on the vileness of men].

Restituer.‡ In that chapter there are some who will find a sad *bill of costs taxed* for them. And among other very true assertions, this is one: *"S'il exige une recompense excessive et disproportionnée à ce qu'il fait, il est obligé à restituer ce qu'il prend de trop."* In plain English: *Excessive fees* must be disgorged by RESTITUTION. It should be thought upon.

There has been an old complaint, *that a good lawyer seldom is a good neighbor.* You know how to confute it, *gentlemen,* by making your *skill in the law,* a blessing to your neighborhood. It was affirmed and foretold as long ago as old *Sallust:* [14] *Sine considicis satis faelices olim fuere, futuraeque sunt urbes.*§ You may, *gentlemen,* if you please, be a vast accession to the *felicity* of your countries.

You shall have some of my PROPOSALS for it, in an historical exhibition. In the Life of Mr. *John Cotton,*[15] there is related this passage concerning his father, who was a *lawyer.*

"That worthy man was very singular, in two most imitable practices. One was, that when any of his neighbors, desirous to sue one another, addressed him for *counsel,* it was his manner, in the most persuasive and obliging terms that could be, to endeavor a *reconciliation* between both parties; preferring the *consolations* of a *peacemaker,* before all the *fees* that he might have got, by blowing up of *differences.* Another was, that every night, it was his custom to *examine himself,* with reflections on the transactions of the day past; wherein if he found, that he had not either *done good* unto others, or *got good* unto his own soul, he would be as much grieved, as ever the famous *Titus* [16] was, when he could complain in the evening, *Amici, diem perdidi."* ‖

What a noble thing would it be for you, to find out oppressed *widows,* and *orphans,* and such as can appear no otherwise than, *in forma pauperis;* objects in whose oppression, *might over-*

‡ Of the cases in which lawyers must make restitution.
§ Without lawyers the towns were and will be quite happy.
‖ Friends, I have lost the day.

comes right; and generously *plead their cause? Deliver the poor and needy, rid them out of the hand of the wicked.* It will be a glorious and a Godlike action!

Wealthy people going to make their *wills,* often ask your advice. You may take the opportunity to advise them, unto such liberalities upon *pious uses,* as may greatly advance the Kingdom of God in the world.

And, when you have an opportunity by *law* to rescue, *the things that are God's,* from the sacrilegious hands of the men that would *rob God,* it is to be hoped, you will do it with all possible generosity and alacrity.

O excellent imitation of our glorious ADVOCATE in the heavens!

Is there nothing to be mended in the *laws?* Perhaps, you may discover many things yet wanting in the *laws; mischiefs* in the execution and application of the *laws,* which ought to be better provided against; *mischiefs* annoying of mankind, against which no *laws* are yet provided. The *reformation of the law,* and more *law* for the *reformation of the world,* is what is mightily called for. I don't say, the *laws* can be so *reduced,* that like those of *Geneva,* five sheets of paper may hold them all; but certainly the *laws* may be so *corrected,* that the world may more sensibly and generally feel the benefit of them. If some *lawyers* that are *men of an excellent spirit,* would employ their thoughts this way, and bring their thoughts to pass in a *parliamentary* way, all the world might fare the better for them. An honest gentleman more than fifty years ago, wrote an, *Examen Legum Angliae,*¶ [17] worthy to be taken at this day, into your consideration.

Your learning often qualifies you to *write excellent things,* not only in your own profession, but also on all the entertaining and edifying themes in the world. The books that have been written by learned *lawyers,* would for number almost equal an

¶ Study of the laws of England.

Alexandrian library. Judge by a *Freherus's* catalogues, or, by a *Prynne's* performances. What rare and rich books, have been written by an *Hale*, by a *Grotius*, and by a *Selden?* [18] Sirs, you may *plead the cause of religion*, and of the *Reformation*, by your well-directed pens; and you may do innumerable services. There is one [19] at this day, who in his *History of the Apostles' Creed*, and his accounts of the *Primitive Church*, has obliged us to say, *that he has offered as a* KING *to the Temple of the King of Heaven.* May the *Lord his God accept* him!

I must now break off.

If you be called, Sir, to the administration of justice, in the quality of a JUDGE, you will prescribe to yourself *rules*, like those, which the renowned Lord Chief Justice *Hale*, so religiously observed, as to become a bright example for all that sit in the seat of judicature. The sum of his, were:

"That justice be administered, *uprightly, deliberately, resolutely.*

"That I rest not on my own *understanding*, but implore the *direction* of GOD.

"That in the execution of justice, I carefully lay aside my own *passions*, and not give way to them, however provoked.

"That I be wholly intent on the business I am about.

"That I suffer not myself to be prepossessed with any judgment at all, till all the business, and both parties are heard."

Of such *methods*, to *do good*, and serve the cause of *righteousness*, and bring on the promised age, wherein the *people shall be righteous*, the very least of all the glorious recompenses, will be the establishment of your profession, in such a *reputation*, as very many incomparable persons in it have deserved; and the most prejudiced people in the world, inquiring after the blemishes of it, must be forced only to bring in an *ignoramus.*[20]

§21. REFORMING SOCIETIES, or *Societies for the Suppression of Disorders*, have begun to grow somewhat into fashion; and it is one of the best *omens* that the world has upon it.[1] *Behold, how great a matter a little* of this heavenly *fire* may kindle! Five or six gentlemen in *London*, began with an heroic resolution, and association, to encounter the torrent of wickedness, which was carrying all before it in the nation. More were soon added unto them; and though they met with great opposition, from *wicked spirits*, and these *incarnate* as well as *invisible*, and some in *high places* too, yet they proceeded with a most honorable and invincible courage. Their *success*, if not proportionable to their *courage*, yet was far from *contemptible*. In the *punishments* inflicted on them who transgressed the laws of *good morality*, there were soon offered many thousands of *sacrifices*, unto the holiness of GOD. Hundreds of *houses* which were the *chambers* of Hell, and the *scandals* of earth, were soon extinguished. There was a remarkable check soon given to raging *profanity;* and the Lord's Day was not openly and horribly profaned as formerly. And among other *essays to do good*, they scattered thousands of *good books*, that had a tendency to reform the evil manners of the people. It was not long before this excellent example was followed in other parts of the *British* Empire. Virtuous men of diverse qualities and persuasions, became the members of the *societies:* persons high and low, Con[forming] and Noncon[forming], united; the union became formidable to the Kingdom of Darkness. The report of the *societies* flew over the seas; the pattern was followed in other countries; men of wisdom in remote parts of *Europe* have made their joyful remark upon them, *that they cause unspeakable good, and annunciate a more illustrious state of the Church of God, which is to be expected, in the conversion of Jews and gentiles. America* too, begins to be irradiated with them!

I will recite an account [2] formerly offered unto the public, of what may be done by such SOCIETIES.

"What incredible advantages would arise unto *religion*, from REFORMING SOCIETIES, if the disposition to them should not fall under unhappy languishments? And if *religion* flourish, and *iniquity* dare no longer show its head, what *prosperity* of every kind, and in everything, would be the consequence: A small SOCIETY may prove an incomparable and invaluable blessing to a town, whose welfare shall become the object of their watchful inquiries: they may be as a *garrison* to defend it from the worst of its enemies: they may quickly render it, *a mountain of holiness, and a dwelling of righteousness*, that shall enjoy the most gracious presence of the Lord. The *Society* may do considerable things towards the execution of wholesome *laws*, whereby *vice* is to be discouraged. *Offenders* against those *laws* may be kept under such a vigilant inspection, that they shall not escape a due *chastisement* for their offenses. The effects of such a chastisement may be, that the rebuked and censured sinners will be reclaimed from their sins; or, however, the judgments of God, which would break forth where such things are indulged, will be diverted. *Ubi judicium, ibi non est judicium.** *Swearing* and *cursing* will not infect the *air;* men will not reel along the streets, turned into *swine* by their *cups.* The cages of *unclean birds* will be dissipated. They whom *idleness* renders dead while they live, will have an honest employment ordered for them, whereby they may earn an honest livelihood. And the *Lord's Day* will visibly be kept *holy to the Lord;* which one thing will soon irradiate a place, with a most lovely *holiness* and *happiness. Vice* is a cowardly thing; it will wonderfully shrink before those that will visibly go to make head against it. If any *laws* to regulate

* Where there is [legal] justice, there is no [divine] judgment [*i.e.,* punishment].

what is amiss, be yet wanting, the *Society* may procure the *legislative power* to be so addressed, that all due provision will soon be made by our law-givers. What is defective in the *by-laws* of the town, may be by the *Society*, so observed, that the town shall be soon advised, and the thing redressed. The choice of such *officers* as may be faithful and useful to the public, may be very much influenced by the *Society*. If any sort of men, are notoriously defective in their duty, the *Society* may by directing *admonitions* and *remonstrances* unto them soon procure the defects to be amended. If any *families* live without *family-worship*, the *Society* may tell their *pastor* of them, and pray him to visit them, and exhort them, and persuade them, to continue no longer in their *paganism* and *atheism;* or, if any are like to be led away by seducers, or other temptations, a care may in this way be taken of them. *Schools* of all kinds, may in many kinds fare the better for the *Society* (and *charity-schools* be erected, inspected, and supported). Books that have in them the *salt* of Heaven, may by means of the *Society* be sprinkled all over the land; and the *savor of Truth* be dispersed about the country. Finally: the *Society* may find out, who are in extreme necessities, and may either by their own liberality, or by that of others to whom they shall commend the matter, obtain succors for the necessitous.

"We know, that a small *society* may do such things, because to our knowledge, it has already done them; and yet, it has been concealed from the knowledge of the world, who they were which did them. And with minds that have any *generosity* or *ingenuity* in them, elevating them above the *dregs of mankind*, there will need no other argument for the production of such a *society*, than the prospect of such excellent things. These are things that will mightily commend themselves unto the thoughts of well-inclined men; and they will easily see it their *honor*, to be of a *society* that will pursue such excellent ends."

The repetition of these passages, is enough to make way for the PROPOSAL:

That a fit number in a neighborhood, whose hearts God has touched with a *zeal to do good*, would combine into a *society*, to meet, when and where they shall agree, and consider that case, "What are the DISORDERS that we may see rising among us? And what may be done, either by ourselves immediately, or by others through our advice, to suppress those disorders?" That they would obtain if they can, the presence of a *minister* with them, and every time they meet, have a *prayer* wherein the glorious Lord shall be called upon, to bless the design, direct and prosper it. That they would also have a *justice of peace*, if it may be, to be a member of the Society. That they once in half a year choose two *stewards*, to dispatch the *business* and *messages* of the *Society*, and manage the *votes* in it; who shall nominate unto the *Society*, their successors, when their term is expired. That they would have a faithful *treasurer*, in whose hands their *stock of charity* may be deposited: and a *clerk*, to keep a convenient *record* of *transactions* and *purposes*. And, finally, that they do with as *modest* and *silent* a conduct as may be, carry on all their undertakings.

In a town accommodated with several such *societies*, it has been an usage, that *once a year*, they have met, all of them together, in one place, and have had a *Day of Prayer*, in which they have *humbled* themselves for doing so little good, and besought the *pardon* of their *unfruitfulness*, through the blood of the *Great Sacrifice;* and implored the *blessing* of Heaven on the *essays to do good*, which they have made, and the *counsel* and *conduct* of Heaven, for their further essays and such influences of Heaven, as may bring about those *reformations*, which it was not in their power to accomplish.

I will finish the PROPOSAL, by reciting the POINTS OF CONSIDERATION which the SOCIETIES may have read unto them from time to time at their meetings, with a due *pause* upon each of them, for anyone to offer what he please upon it.

I. "Is there any REMARKABLE DISORDER in the place that requires our endeavor for the suppression of it? And in what good, fair, likely way may we endeavor it?

II. "Is there any PARTICULAR PERSON, whose *disorderly behaviors* may be so scandalous and so notorious, that we may do well to send unto the said person our charitable *admonitions?* Or, are there any *contending persons*, whom we should admonish, to quench their *contentions?*

III. "Is there any *special service* to the interest of religion, which we may conveniently desire our MINISTERS, to take notice of?

IV. "Is there anything, which we may do well to mention and recommend unto the JUSTICES, for the further promoting of *good order?*

V. "Is there any sort of OFFICERS among us, to such a degree unmindful of their duty, that we may do well to mind them of it?

VI. "Can any further methods be devised, that *ignorance* and *wickedness* may be more chased from our people in general? And that HOUSEHOLD-PIETY in particular, may flourish among them?

VII. "Does there appear any instance of OPPRESSION or FRAUDULENCE, in the *dealings* of any sort of people, that may call for our essays, to get it rectified?

VIII. "Is there any matter to be humbly moved unto the LEGISLATIVE POWER to be enacted into a LAW for public benefit?

IX. "Do we know of any person languishing under sad and sore AFFLICTION; and is there anything that we may do, for the succor of such an afflicted neighbor?

X. "Has any person any PROPOSAL to make, for our own further advantage and assistance, that we ourselves may be in a probable and regular capacity, to pursue the INTENTIONS before us?"

My reader, *look now towards Heaven, and tell the stars, if thou be able to number them,* which the *telescopes* have already discovered, and are still to fetch into their discovery, besides the *nineteen hundred,* which are brought down into the *later globes;* yea, tell first the leaves of an *Hercynian* forest, and the *drops* of an *Atlantic* Ocean; then tell how many *good things* may be done, by SOCIETIES of good men, having such *points of consideration* always before them!

And yet, when such SOCIETIES have done all the good they can and nothing but good, and walk on in a more unspotted *brightness* than that of the *moon in heaven,* let them look to be maligned, and libelled; as: *a set of scoundrels, who are maintained by lying, serve God for unrighteous gain, and ferret whores for subsistence, and are not more unanimous against immorality in their informations, than for it in their practice: avoid no sins in themselves, and will suffer none in anybody else.* I suppose, they that publish their censures on the *manners of the age* will express this malignity, because they *have* done so. Sirs, *add to your faith, courage,* and be armed for such trials of it!

[CHAPTER TWELVE: DESIDERATA]

§22. We will not propose, that our *essays to do good*, should ever come to an end. But we will now put an end unto this, of tendering PROPOSALS for it. It shall conclude with a *catalogus desideratorum*, or a mention of some obvious, and general *services* for the Kingdom of God among mankind, whereto 'twere to be desired, that religious and ingenious men might be awakened.

A CATALOGUE OF DESIRABLES, waiting for the *zeal of good men* to prosecute them.

(*Difficilem rem optas; generis humani innocentiam!*) †

I. The propagation of the holy and glorious *religion of* CHRIST; a religion which *emancipates* mankind from the worst of slaveries and miseries, and wonderfully *ennobles* it; and which alone prepares men for the blessedness of another world: why is this no more endeavored by the professors of it? PROTESTANTS, why will you be out-done by *popish idolaters!* Oh! the vast pains which those *bigots*, have taken, to carry on the *Romish* merchandises and idolatries! No less than six hundred clergymen, in that one order of the *Jesuits*, did within a few years, at several times, embark themselves for *China*, to win over that mighty nation unto their bastard-Christianity. No less than five hundred of them lost their *lives*, in the difficulties of their enterprise; and yet the survivors go on with it; expressing a sort of trouble, that it fell not unto their share to make a sacrifice of their *lives*, in enterprising the propagation of religion. *O my God, I am ashamed, and blush to lift up my face unto thee my God!* It were but a *Christian*, but a *grateful*, but an *equal* thing; but who

† You choose a difficult thing, the righteousness of mankind.

138

can foretell what *prosperity* might be the recompense! If
our *companies* and *factories*, would set apart a more considerable part of their *gains* for this work, and set upon a more
vigorous prosecution of it.[1] *Gordon's* [2] proposal, unto all men
of estates, to set apart a small part of their estates for this
purpose (at the end of his *Geography*), should be taken into
further consideration. What has been done by the *Dutch*
missionaries at *Ceylon*, and what is doing by the *Danish* missionaries at *Malabar*, one would think, might animate us, to
imitate them!

If men of a spirit for *evangelizing*, and *illuminating* a woeful world, would learn the *languages* of some nations that are
yet *ungospellized*, and wait on the Providence of Heaven, to
lead them to, and own them in, some *apostolical undertakings*,
who can tell what might be done? We know, what *Ruffinus*
relates concerning the conversion of the *Iberians;* and what
Socrates, concerning the things done by *Frumentius* and
Ædesius, in the *inner India*.[3]

But on this *desirable* there are two things *remarkable*.

First, it is the conjecture of some *seers*, that until the
Temple be *cleansed*, there will be no general appearance of
the *nations* to worship in it. And the truth is, there will be
danger, until then, that many persons active in *Societies for
the Propagation of Religion*, may be more intent upon propa-
gating their own little *forms* and *fancies* and *interests*, than
the more *weighty matters of the Gospel*. Yea, 'twill be well,
if they be not unawares imposed upon, to hurt *Christianity*
where 'tis well-established, while places wholly *ungospellized*
in the neighborhood may lie neglected. Let us therefore do
what we can towards the Church's *reformation*, in order to
its *dilatation*.

Secondly, it is probable, that the *Holy Spirit* in operations,
like those of the first ages, whereby Christianity was first
planted, will be again conferred from our *ascended Lord*, for

the *spreading* of it. The *Holy Spirit*, who has withdrawn from the *apostate church*, will come, and *abide* with us, and render this world like a *watered garden*. His irresistible influences, will cause whole *nations* to be *born at once;* He will not only *convert* but *unite*, His people. By Him, God shall *dwell with men*. Would not the *Heavenly Father give His Holy Spirit*, if it were more *asked* of Him!

II. 'Tis lamentable to see the *ignorance* and *wickedness*, yet remaining, even in many parts of the *British* dominions: in *Wales;* in the *Highlands;* and in *Ireland*. Are the *Gouges* all dead? There are pretended *shepherds*, in the world, that will never be able to answer before the Son of God, for their laying so little to heart, the *deplorable* circumstances, of so many people, whom they might, if they were not scandalously negligent, bring to be more acquainted with the only Saviour. And there might be more done, that some of the *American* colonies, may no longer be such *Cimmerian* ones.

III. Why is no more done, for the poor *Greeks*, and *Armenians*, and *Muscovites*, and other Christians, who have little *preaching*, and no *printing* among them? If we sent *Bibles*, and *Psalters*, and other *books of piety* among them, in their own languages, they would be *noble* presents, and, God knows, how *useful* ones!

IV. Poor *sailors*, and poor *soldiers*, call for our pity. They meet with *great and sore troubles*. Their *manners* are too commonly such, as discover no very good effects of their *troubles*. What shall be done to make them a *better sort of men?* There must, besides more *books of piety* distributed among them, other methods be thought upon; *Cadit asinus et est qui sublevat. Perit anima, et non est qui manum apponat!* ‡ Let *Austin* awaken us.

V. The *Tradesman's Library* needs to be more enriched. We have seen, *Husbandry Spiritualized;* ⁴ and, *Shepherdy*

‡ An ass falls, and there is someone to help lift him up. A soul dies, and there is no one to help it.

Spiritualized; and, *Navigation Spiritualized;* we have seen, the *weaver* also accommodated, with agreeable meditations. To spread the *nets of salvation* for men, in the ways of their *personal callings,* and convey good thoughts unto them, in the *terms* and *steps,* of their daily business, is a real service to the interests of piety. A BOOK also, that shall be an *onomatologia monitoria,* and shall advise people how to make their *names* become unto them, the *monitors* of their duty; might be of much use to the *Christened* world. And, a BOOK, that shall be, *The Angel of Bethesda,* and shall instruct people how to improve in agreeable points of piety, from the several maladies, which their *bodies* may be diseased withal; and at the same time, inform them of the most experimented, natural, specific *remedies* for their diseases, might be very useful to mankind. These two subjects, if not undertaken by any other hand, may be so shortly by that which now writes; [5] except the glorious Lord of my life, immediately put an end unto it; and *my days are past, my purposes are broken off, even the thoughts of my heart!*

VI. *Universities* that shall have more *collegia pietatis* in them, like those of the excellent *Franckius* [6] in the lower *Saxony;* oh! that there were more of them!—*seminaries* in which the scholars may have a most polite education; but not be sent forth with recommendations for the evangelical ministry, till it be upon a strict examination found, that their souls are fired with the *fear* of God, and the *love* of Christ, and a *zeal* to do good, and a *resolution* to bear poverty, and obloquy, and all sorts of temptations, in the service of our holy religion; they would be the *wonders* of the world, and what *wonders* might they do in the world!

Let the *charity-schools* also, *increase and multiply; charity-schools,* which may provide subjects for the great Saviour, blessings for the next generation; *charity-schools,* not perverted unto the ill purposes of introducing a *defective Christianity.*

VII. Those things, that so far as we *understand by the books* of the sacred Prophecies, are to be, *the works of our day;* 'Tis *wisdom* to observe and pursue. When the time was arrived, that the *Antichrist* must enter his last *half-time,* one poor monk proves a main instrument of ravishing *half* his empire from him. Thus to fall in with the designs of the *Divine Providence,* is the way to be wonderfully prospered and honored. One small man, thus *nicking the time* for it, may do wonders!

I take the *works of our day* to be:

1. The *reviving of primitive Christianity;* to study and restore everything, of the *primitive* character. The *apostasy* is going off. The time for *cleansing the Temple* comes on. More *Edwardses* [7] would be vast blessings, where the *primitive doctrines of Christianity* are depraved.

2. The persuading of the *European* powers, to shake off the chains of *popery.* This argument—there is no *popish nation,* but what by embracing the *Protestant religion,* would *ipso facto,* not only assert themselves into a glorious *liberty,* but also *double their wealth* immediately—'tis marvellous, that it is no more yet hearkened unto! Sirs, prosecute it, with more of *demonstration.* One shows, that the abolishing of popery in *England,* is worth at least eight millions of pounds yearly to the nation. Let the argument be tried with other nations, the argument, *ab utili.*

3. The *forming* and *quickening* of that PEOPLE, that are to be, THE STONE CUT OUT OF THE MOUNTAIN. Here, as well as in some other things, *none of the wicked shall understand, but the wise shall understand.* God will do His own work, in His own time, and in His own way. And *Austin* tells me, *Utile est ut taceatur aliquod verbum, propter incapaces.*§

§ It is prudent to refrain from speaking some words to men who are incapable of understanding.

[CHAPTER THIRTEEN:] THE CONCLUSION

The *zeal of the Lord of Hosts will perform these things:* a *zeal* inspired and produced by the *Lord of Hosts* in His faithful servants, will put them upon the performance of such things. Nothing has been yet proposed, that is impracticable; *Non fortia loquor, sed possibilia.*‖ But, *Eusebius* has taught me, *Vere magnum est magna facere, et teipsum putare nihil.*¶ Sirs, under and after a course of such *actions*, which have a true glory in them, and really are more glorious than all the *actions* and *achievements*, whereof those bloody plunderers, whom we call *conquerors*, have made a wretched ostentation: and perhaps made inscriptions like those of *Pompey* [1] on his Temple of *Minerva*—still *humility*, must be the *crown* of all. All, nothing without *humility*; nothing without a sense that you are *nothing*, a consent to be made *nothing*. You must first, most humbly acknowledge unto the great GOD, *that after you have done all, you are unprofitable servants;* and make your humble confession, that not only you have *done but that which was your duty to do*, but also that you have exceedingly fallen short of doing your *duty*. If God abase you with very *dark dispensations* of His Providence, after all your indefatigable and your disinterested essays to *glorify* Him, humble yourselves before Him; yet abate nothing of your *essays*; hold on, saying, "My God will humble me, yet will I glorify Him. Lord, Thou art righteous; but still I will do all I can to serve thy glorious Kingdom." This indeed, is a more easy *humiliation;* but then there is one to be demanded, of much greater difficulty: that is, that you humbly

‖ I speak not of difficult things but of possibilities.
¶ It is certainly noble to do great things and to think nothing of yourself.

submit unto all the *diminutions*, among *men*, that God shall order for you. Your admirable Saviour was one who *went about* ever *doing of good;* mankind was never visited by such a *benefactor*. And yet we read, "He was One spoken against." Never anyone so vilified! Had He been the worst *malefactor* in the world, He could not have been worse dealt withal. He expostulated, "For which of my good works is it that you treat me so?" Yet they went on; they hated Him, they reproached Him, they murdered Him. *Austin* said very truly, *Remedium elationis est contuitus Dominicae crucis.** It will also be the remedy of discouragement; it will keep you from *sinking*, as well as being *lifted up*. You are conformed unto your Saviour, in your watchful endeavors to *do good*, and be *fruitful in every good work*. But your conformity unto Him, yet *lacks one thing;* that is, after all, to be *despised and rejected of men;* and patiently to bear the contempt, and malice, and abuses of an *untoward generation*. One of the fathers, who sometimes wanted a little of this grace, could say, *Nihil est quod nos ita et hominibus et Deo gratos facit, quam si vitae merito magni, et humilitate infimi simus.*† 'Tis an excellent thing to come to *nothing*. If you hear the hopes of disaffected men, to see you *come to nothing, hear* it with as much of satisfaction as they can *hope* it. Embrace *exinanitions;* embrace *annihilations*. I find a zealous and famous *doer of good*, much affected with the picture of a devout man, to whom a voice comes down from Heaven, *Quid vis fieri pro te?* Whereto he replies, *Nihil, Domine, nisi pati et contemni pro te.*‡ Sirs, let it be seen somewhere else than in *picture;* be you the *substance* of it. Thus, *let patience have its perfect work!*

I hope, you have more discretion, than to imagine, that because you are never *weary of well-doing*, therefore you

---

* The remedy for pride is the contemplation of the Cross.

† Nothing makes us more pleasing to God and men than being low in humility even if we achieve greatness in our lives.

‡ What do you want me to do for you? . . . Nothing, Lord, but that I may suffer and be despised for your sake.

should be universally *well-spoken of*. No; 'twill be just the contrary. To *do well*, and to *hear ill*, is the common experience, and ought to be our constant expectation. For this most *unreasonable* thing, there are very many *reasons*. 'Twill be impossible to *do much good*, but some or other will count themselves *hurt* by what you do. You will unavoidably serve some *interests*, which others are indisposed unto. 'Tis also in the nature of *madmen*, to take up strange prejudices against their *best friends;* to be set against none so much as *them*. Now, we may everywhere see those, concerning whom we are told, *madness is in their hearts*. It will appear in their being unaccountably prejudiced, against those that most of all seek to *do good* unto them. Then, *he teareth me in his wrath who hateth me; he gnasheth upon me with his teeth, mine enemy sharpeneth his eyes upon me!* [2] Then, to *skorakizing* a *benefactor*, for nothing in the world but because he would have been so! He shall be honored, as the *Lindians* worshipped *Hercules*, by *cursing*, and throwing of *stones*. The *wrath* of God, against a sinful and woeful world, has likewise its operation in this grievous matter. If men always upon *intentions* and *inventions* to *do good*, were so generally beloved and esteemed as they might be, they would be *instruments* of doing more *good*, than the justice of Heaven, can yet allow to be done for *such* a world. *The world is not worthy* of them, nor of that *good* that is endeavored by them. To deprive the world of that *good*, they must be left unto a strange *aversion* for those men that would fain do it. This cripples them, fetters them, defeats their excellent purposes! Nor is the *Devil* idle on this occasion. A man who shall *do much good*, will therein do much *harm* unto the empire of the *Devil*. It would be much, if the *Devil* should not *seek to devour*, or take an exquisite revenge upon such *men of God*. Except God lay an uncommon restraint upon that *wicked one*, such is the *power of the Adversary*, and such an *energy* the *Devil* has upon the minds of multitudes, that he will notably and bitterly *re-*

venge himself upon any notable *doer of good;* and procure him a *troop* of enemies, three volleys of obloquies. But, O servant of God, *by Him thou wilt run through a troop; by thy God thou wilt leap over a wall.*[3] We may be so far from wondering, that *wicked men* are violently disaffected unto a man who does abundance of *good,* and spread as many stories, and write as many libels, to his disadvantage, as ever the incomparable *Calvin* suffered from them; we may rather wonder that the *Devil* does not make this world hotter than a *Babylonish furnace* for him; too hot for his abiding in it. Sirs, if you will *do much,* 'tis very likely that the *Devil* may sometimes raise upon your opportunities to *do good,* such an *horrible tempest,* as may threaten a total ruin unto them. You may fear that you see your *serviceableness,* the *apple of your eye struck out;* you may be driven to prayers, to tears, to *fasting often* in secret places; prostrate in the dust, you must *offer up your supplications, with strong crying and tears,* to Him that is *able to save* your opportunities from *death;* you must cry out, "O deliver my soul (my serviceableness), from the sword, my darling (my serviceableness), from the power of the Dog!"

The words of the great *Baxter,*[4] are proper and worthy to be introduced on this occasion.

"The *temptations* and *suggestions* of *Satan,* yea, and oft his external contrived snares are such, as frequently give men a palpable discovery of his agency. Whence is it, that such wonderful successive trains of impediments, are set in the way of almost any man, that intends any great and good work in the world? I have among men of my own acquaintance observed such admirable frustrations of many designed excellent works, by such strange unexpected means, and such variety of them, and so powerfully carried on, as hath of itself convinced me, that there is a most vehement invisible malice permitted by God to resist mankind, and to militate against all good in the world. Let a man have any work of greatest natural importance, which tends to no great benefit to mankind, and he may go on with it, without any extraordinary impedition. But let him have any great design for *common good*, in things that tend to destroy sin, to heal divisions, to revive charity, to increase virtue, to save men's souls; yea, or to the public common felicity; and his impediments shall be so multifarious, so far-fetched, so subtle, so incessant, and in despite of all his care and resolution, usually so successful, that he shall seem to himself, to be like a man that is held fast hand and foot, while he sees no one touch him; or that sees an hundred blocks brought and cast before him in his way, while he sees no one to do it."

I transcribe this passage for this purpose. O doer of good, expect a conflict with *wicked spirits in high places*, to clog all the good thou dost propose to do; and expect that restless endeavors of theirs, to overwhelm thee with vile *ideas* in the minds, and *calumnies* in the mouths, of many people concerning thee, will be some of their *devices* to defeat all thy *proposals*. *Be not ignorant of the Satanic devices!*

Yea, and if the *Devil* were asleep, there is malignity enough, in the hearts of *wicked men* themselves, to render a man that will *do good*, very distasteful and uneasy to them. They are the offspring of him, who *slew his brother, because his works were righteous;*[5] and they will malign a man, because he is useful to other men. Indeed, *Malis displicere est laudari:* § but wicked men, will *curse* a man, because he is a *blessing*. Oh! base and black disposition!

I happened once to be present in the room, where a dying man could not die till he had bewailed unto a minister whom he had now therefore sent for,[6] the unjust *calumnies* and *injuries* which he had often cast upon him: the minister asked the poor penitent, what was the occasion of his *abusiveness;* whether he had been by any misreports imposed upon? The man made this horrible answer: "No, Sir; 'twas nothing but this: I thought you

§ To displease the wicked is to be praised.

were a good man, and that you did much good in the world, and therefore I hated you! Oh! Is it possible, is it possible," said the poor sinner, "for such a sinner to find a pardon!" Truly, though other causes may be pretended for the *spite* and *rage* of wicked men, against a *fruitful doer of good;* yet I shall not be *deceived*, if I fear, that oftentimes a secret *antipathy* to the *Kingdom of God*, lies at the bottom of it. Or it may be sometimes a *pale envy*, in proud men, raging that other men are more *useful* in the world than they, and vexing themselves with worse than *Sicilian torments*, at the sight of what God and man do for other men. *They see it and are grieved.* Sirs, *Non bonus est qui non ad invidiam usque bonus est.*‖ But now, for such causes, you must not *think strange of the trial*, if men *speak evil of you*, after you have *done good* unto many, yea, unto those very people who *speak* it. It will not be *strange*, if you should *hear the defaming of many;* if the men who do not love the *holy ways* of the Lord in His churches, have no love to you; if never so many *Aristophaneses* [7] fall upon you; if *javelins* are thrown at you, with a rage reaching to Heaven; and if *pamphlets* are stuffed with vile figments and slanders upon you. God may wisely permit these things, and in much faithfulness, *to hide pride from you.* (*O quantum est venenum superbiae, quod non potest nisi veneno curari!*) ¶ Alas, while we carry the *grave-clothes* of *pride* still about us, these rough hands are the best that can be to pull them off! If you should meet with such things, you must bear them with much *meekness*, much *silence*, great *self-abhorrence*, and a spirit to *forgive*, the worst of all your persecutors. *Being defamed*, you must *entreat.* Be glad, if you can redeem any opportunities to *do good.* Be ready to *do good*, even unto those from whom you *suffer evil.* And when you have done all the *good* that you can, reckon yourself well

‖ He who does not provoke envy is not good.
¶ Oh, how great is the poison of pride, which cannot be cured but with poison!

paid, if you escape as well as the *crane* did from the *wolf*, and if you are not *punished* for what you do. In short, be insensible of any *merits* in your performances. Lie in the *dust*, and be willing that both GOD and *man* should lay you there. Have your spirit reconciled unto *indignities*. Entertain them with all the *calmness*, all the *temper*, imaginable. Be content, that *three hundred in Sparta*, should be preferred before you. When envious people can fix no other blemish on you, they will say of you, as they said of *Cyprian*,[8] that *you are a proud man;* because you do not jog on in their heavy road of *slothfulness*. Bear this also, with yet a more profound *humility*. 'Tis the last effort usually made by the dying *pride of life*, to bear the charge of *pride* impatiently, with a *proud* impatience.

Ye *useful men*, your *acceptance* with your Saviour, and with God through your Saviour, and *recompense* in the world to come, is to carry you cheerfully through all your *essays* at *usefulness*. To be *reprobate for every good work*, is a character, from which 'twill be the *wisdom* of all men, to fly with all the dread imaginable. But then, to be *always abounding in the work for the Lord*, this is always the truest and the highest *wisdom*. 'Tis the *wisdom which is from above*, that is full of *mercy and good fruits*. The *sluggards* who do no good in the world, are *wise in their own conceit;* but the men who are diligent in *doing of good*, can give such a *reason* for what they do, as proves them to be *really wise*. Men *leave off to be wise*, when they *leave off to do good*.[9] The *wisdom* of it appears in this: 'tis the best way of spending our *time;* 'tis *well-spent*, when spent in *doing of good*. It is also a sure way, a sweet way, effectually to bespeak the *blessings* of God on ourselves. Who so likely to *find blessings*, as the men that *are blessings?* It has been said, *Qui bene vivit, semper orat;* * so I will say, *Qui bene agit, bene orat.*†
Every *action* we do for the *Kingdom* of God, is in the efficacy

* He who lives well is always praying.
† He who does good, prays well.

BONIFACIUS

of it, a *prayer* for the *kindness* of God. While we are *at work* for God, certainly, He will be *at work* for us, and ours: He will do for us, more than ever we have *done* for Him; far *more than we can ask or think!* There is a *voice* in every *good thing* that is done; 'tis that, *Oh! do good unto them that are good!* Thus my BONIFACIUS anon comes to wear the name of BENEDICTUS also. Yea, and there may be this more particular effect of what we do. While we *employ* our *wits* for the interests of God, it is very probable, that we shall *sharpen* them for our own. We shall become the more *wise for ourselves,* because we have been *wise to do good.* And of the man who is a *tree that brings forth fruit,* we read, *whatsoever he doth shall prosper.*[10] Nor can a man take a readier way to *live joyfully, all the days of the life of our vanity, which God has given us under the sun.* For, now our *life* will not be thrown away in *vanity;* we don't *live in vain.* My friend, *go thy way* and be joyful; *for God accepteth thy works.* Our *few* and *evil* days, are made much less so, by our *doing* of *good* in every one of them, as it rolleth over us. Yea, the Holy *Spirit* of God who is the *quickener* of them who *do good without ceasing,* will be their *comforter.* Every day of our *activity* for the Kingdom of God, will be in some sort a day of *Pentecost* unto us, a day of the Holy Spirit's coming upon us. The *consolations of God,* will *not be small,* with the man, who is full of *contrivances for God,* and for His Kingdom. In short, we read, "The valleys are covered over with corn; they shout for joy, they also sing." We may be in *low* circumstances: but if we abound in the fruits of *well-doing,* and if we feed many with our services, we are *covered over with corn.* We shall *shout for joy, and also sing,* if we be so. The *conscience* of what we do, and of what we aim to do, will be a *continual feast* unto us. *Our rejoicing is this, the testimony of our conscience!* And, *Recte fecisse merces est.*‡ Yea, the *pleasure* in doing of *good offices,* 'tis inexpressible; 'tis unparalleled; 'tis *angelical;* more to be

‡ Virtue is its own reward.

150

envied than any *sensual pleasure;* a most *refined* one. Pleasure was long since defined, *the result of some excellent action.* 'Tis, a sort of *holy Epicurism.* O most *pitiable* they that will continue strangers to it! But, *memineris,* was the constant word of encouragement unto a soldier. I say, *remember;* there's more to be *remembered.*

When the *serviceable* man comes to his *Nunc Dimittis,*§ then, he who did *live desired,* shall *die lamented.* It shall be witnessed and remembered of him, *that he was one who did good in Israel.* An *epitaph* the glory whereof is beyond that of the most superb and stately *pyramid!* When [*i.e.*, then] the calumniators, who once *licked the file* of his reputation, shall have only the impotence of their defeated malice to reflect upon. And a *Thersites* [11] will not have a more disadvantageous article in all his character than this, *that he was an enemy to such an* Ulysses. But what shall be done for this good man in the *Heavenly world?* His *part* and his *work* in the *City of God,* is as yet incomprehensible unto us. But the *kindness* that his God will show unto him, in the *strong City,* will be *marvelous! marvelous!* To make the exclamation of *Austin,* writing, *of the City: Quanta erit illa faelicitas, ubi nullum erit malum, nullum latebit bonum!* ‖ His essays to fill this world with *righteous things,* are so many *tokens for good* upon him, that he shall have a *share* and a *work,* in that world, wherein shall *dwell* nothing but *righteousness.* He shall be introduced into that world, with a word from the mouth of the glorious JESUS, which will be worth a thousand worlds: *Well done, good and faithful servant!* —And, oh! what shall be done for him! He has done what he could for the *honor of the King of Heaven;* all shall be done for him, that may be done for one whom the *King of Heaven delights to honor.*

§ Permission to depart—that is, his death—in contentment that he has done all he can do.

‖ How great the happiness will be, where there will be no evil and no good will be hidden!

I will give you all summed up in one word: it is that, Prov. 14. 22., MERCY AND TRUTH SHALL BE TO THEM WHO DEVISE GOOD. Children of God, there is a strain of *mercy and truth*, in all the *good* that you *devise*. You *devise* how to deal *mercifully* and *truly*, with everyone; and bring everyone to do so too. And the *mercy* and *truth* of God, now forever engaged for you, shall here suffer you to *lack no good thing*, but shall hereafter do you *good* beyond what the *heart of man*, can yet *conceive*. A *faithful God*, a Saviour who is one *of great faithfulness*, is He that has *promised* it! *The mouth of the Lord hath spoken it.*

I have not forgotten the words used by the excellent *Calvin*, when the order for his banishment from ungrateful *Geneva* was brought unto him. *Certe si hominibus servivissem, mala mihi merces persolveretur; sed bene est, quod ei inservivi, qui nunquam non servis suis rependit, quod semel promisit.*¶ And I will conclude with a TESTIMONY [12] that I shall abide by. 'Tis this: were a man able to write in *seven languages:* could he converse daily with the sweets of all the *liberal sciences,* that more polite men ordinarily pretend unto; did he entertain himself with all ancient and modern *histories;* and could he feast continually on the *curiosities* which all sorts of learning may bring unto him; none of all this would afford the ravishing satisfaction, much less would any grosser delights of the *senses* do it; which he might find, in relieving the distresses of a poor, mean, *miserable neighbor;* and which he might much more find, in doing any *extensive service* for the Kingdom of our great SAVIOUR in the world; or anything to redress the miseries under which mankind is generally languishing.

¶Certainly, if I depended on men, I would be paid a bad reward for it; but it is all right, because I have served Him who has never failed to pay His servants what He had once promised.

AN APPENDIX,

Concerning the ESSAYS that are made, for the PROPAGATION OF RELIGION among the Indians, in the *Massachusetts* Province of NEW ENGLAND.

It has been desired, that our Book of ESSAYS TO DO GOOD, may give an account, of some that are actually pursued, on one of the most important articles that have been proposed. The occasion for this desire, has been given by some odd insinuations made by some who express a zeal for, *the propagation of religion*, as if nothing had been done that way, by any people of our profession, who readily own, "That we are for embracing and diffusing the holy religion of CHRIST, in the *original purity* wherein His Gospel has given it unto us, without humane *additions* and *inventions*." 'Tis true, we have cause always to blame ourselves for our own *deficiencies* in such a work of God. And if we give an account of what we have done, it must be with an holy shame that we have *done so little*. *Pride*, and *vainglorious ostentation*, be thou at all possible distance from the *relation*, which our concern to have the grace of God acknowledged, and a well-designing society of good men defended from injurious imputations, has compelled us to communicate unto the world.

It shall be done with all the *modesty* and *brevity* that the matter will allow of.

In the book entitled, *Magnalia Christi Americana*,[1] or, THE HISTORY OF NEW-ENGLAND, there is a large account of what

153

was *formerly done*, for the Christianizing of our *Indians*. Thither we refer the reader, for all that was *formerly done:* which when he reads, he will certainly wish for more Eliots in the world. *The present state of Christianity* among them, is what must now be reported.

The number of *Indians* in this land, is not comparable to what it was, in the middle of the former century. The wars which after an offered and rejected Gospel, they perfidiously began upon the English, above thirty years ago, brought a quick desolation upon whole nations of them. All that remain under the English influences in the *Massachusetts* Province, are generally recovered out of their paganism, to some sense of the *Christian religion*.

The Christianized Indians on the two islands of *Martha's* Vineyard, and *Nantucket* make a very considerable body. At *Martha's* Vineyard and *Elizabeth's* Islands, there are ten congregations, in which a glorious Christ is worshipped. There are two Englishmen, and ten Indians, that are preachers to them, in their own language. They have *schools* also, in which their children are taught to read and write; and know the Catechism. At *Nantucket*, there are at least three congregations; and more than as many preachers.

From these *islands* we will pass to the adjacent *continent*, where a careful inquiry has been lately made, in a *visitation* ordered for that purpose by the commissioners for such affairs. The result of the inquiry was, that there are between twenty and thirty congregations of *Christianized Indians*, here on the *main;* whereto there belong near three thousand souls. Here are ten English preachers, who give them their instructions and assistances, and preach unto them, either on the *Lord's days*, or in appointed *lectures*. There are also between twenty and thirty *Indian* teachers, by whom the exercises of the *Lord's days* are mostly managed. They have in several of these villages on the *main*, also made handsome subscriptions of their own, towards the building of *meetinghouses;* wherein the English likewise have helped them. They have the whole *Bible* in their own language; which has been here twice printed for them. This *great light* has been *satellited*, with other books which we have also printed for them, in their own language. Their library is continually growing, by *new books*, wherewith we serve and suit the interests of Christianity among them, from time to time, as we see occasion. And their *schools* are multiplying. *Family prayer* also is frequently upheld among them. And their *marriages* are usually celebrated according to the directions left by the famous ELIOT, whose name still is of much authority with them.

There are some congregations of *Indians*, which are not advanced unto all the privileges of the *evangelical church-state*; not yet combining for, and enjoying of, all *special ordinances*. Yet a considerable number of them are so; and some *new churches* have been lately formed and filled among them.

The performances in the ordinary congregations of the *Indians*, have been often such, that there are very many English witnesses, who have not a little admired at the gravity, the attention, the affection expressed in them. The pertinent *prayers* and (*sine monitore, quia de pectore*) the orthodox *sermons* (at the hearing whereof, the very children of a dozen years old will readily turn to the proofs), and the singing of *psalms*, with a melody outdoing many of the English, in their meetings, have been frequently observed with admiration. To see such forlorn savages, and the most rueful ruins of mankind, not only *cicurated* into some civility, but also *elevated* unto so much knowledge and practice of *Christianity*, has to some appeared an amiable and admirable spectacle!

In their churches, they have *pastors* and *elders* of their own; *ordained*, sometimes by the hands of *English* ministers; and sometimes by the hands of the *Indian* ministers, in the presence of the English; all after the solemn English manner. And by *admonitions* and *excommunications* publicly dispensed, they proceed against scandalous offenders: for which intent, and that they may seasonably find and heal all *scandals*, they hold a *church meeting* the week before every Communion.

One that is at this time, a pious and faithful English minister, but preaching also to the *Indians*, has given in unto us, this testimony:

"Their gravity, and diligent attendance in the time of worship, with the affectionate confessions of such as are admitted, into the church, make me hope, that many of them may have the work of the Spirit wrought in them, *according to the working of the mighty power of God.* Their method, respecting those that are admitted into their communion, is more according to the manner of the churches in the primitive times, than is now practiced among the churches in most parts. The person to be admitted, stands forth in the midst of the assembly; and first makes a *declaration* of his *knowledge*, and sometimes desires *information* in things more arduous and doubtful. And then, he makes a *confession of sin;* which they do (as I have seen) with *tears* and *trembling*, like him in the *sixteenth* chapter of the *Acts*. And then he gives an account of *experiences* he has had, of convictions, awakenings, and comforts; in which they are large and particular. After which (much counsel and exhortation, to remain steadfast in the *faith* and *ways* of the Lord, being given them, by their *pastor* and *elder*) they are admitted. I would (and not ungroundedly) hope, that *additions* are *made unto the Church daily of such as shall be saved.* There are many, which maintain a Christian conversation, and are to be accounted, not *almost*, but *altogether Christians*. And this does encourage the preaching of the *Gospel* to them; when we see, it pleases God to make it, *His power unto salvation.*"

At present, we can do nothing for those bloody savages in the *Eastern parts*, who have been taught by the *French priests*, that the Virgin *Mary* was a *French* lady, and that our great Saviour was a *Frenchman*, and that the *English* murdered Him, and that He rose from the dead, and is taken up to the heavens, but that all that would recommend themselves to His favor, must revenge His quarrel on the English people; which issuing out from their indiscoverable swamps, they have often done with cruel depredations. When we have had the short respites of a truce with them, we have made several new attempts to carry them the tenders of a *glorious Gospel;* but they have presently broke out into fresh hostilities, which have put an end unto all good expectations concerning them.

AN APPENDIX

There has been *something done* to *Christianize* the *Mohegans*, and other Indians, in the Colony of *Connecticut;* but, *Lord, who has believed!* They have been obstinate in their paganism; however their obstinacy has not put an end unto our endeavors.

An exemplary Indian minister, whose name is *Japhet*, has of late years made several sallies, among his pagan countrymen, about the *Narragansett* country; and the *hand of the Lord has been with him*, and many *have believed, and turned unto the Lord*.

We have made many trials, to make the *joyful sound* of the Gospel, reach unto the Five Nations, that are some hundreds of miles distant from us, to the westward. All that is yet accomplished, is, to support and reward the pains of several *Dutch* ministers, who proceed as far as they well can, that these may no longer be such *foolish nations;* and have seen some comfortable successes of their ministry.

The principal concern for the Indians in the *Massachusetts* Province, is to preserve and improve the *Christianity* already professed among them, and prevent the loss of a *noble work* by some degeneracies, which have no very well-boding aspect upon it: especially, to prevent the fatal effects, with which the *bottle* threatens it. In order hereto, various methods are used continually, to keep a watchful inspection on their manners, and to make what progress we can in *Anglicizing* of them. These things are in the *practice* encumbered with difficulties, beyond what can be by most men in the bare *theory* imagined. But the *commissioners* here entrusted, for the management of that affair, continually consult and pursue, what may be most subservient unto the grand intention.

ADVERTISEMENT

It is a passage of the incomparable BOYLE: "When I consider, how much more to the advantage of the Sacred Writings, and of Christian theology in general, diverse texts have been explained and discoursed of, by the excellent *Grotius, Masius, Mede,* and Sir *Francis Bacon,*[1] and some other late great wits (to name now no living ones), in their several kinds, than the same places have been handled by vulgar expositors, and other divines; and when I consider, that none of these worthies was at once a great philosopher and a great critic; I cannot but hope, that when it shall please God, to stir up persons of a philosophical genius, well furnished with critical learning, and the principles of true philosophy, and shall give them an hearty concern for the advance of His truths, these men will make explications, and discoveries that shall be admirable. You should no more measure the wisdom of God couched in the Bible, by the glosses and systems of common expositors and preachers, than estimate the wisdom He has expressed in the contrivance of the world, by *Magirus's* or *Eustachius's* Physics."[2]

Many years after this, the admirable *Witsius*[3] comforts us with a passage of an observable aspect that way: "*Neque profecto officio hic suo defuerunt illustres animae.* There have not been wanting those illustrious men, who have observed all the solid discoveries in *philosophy,* all the curious researches of *antiquity,* or that has occurred in *physics* or in *law,* relating to the *Sacred Scriptures,* and have applied it all with a signal dexterity to the *illustration* thereof; and so 'tis come to pass, that *theology,* which had vast riches of its own before, is now also enriched with foreign *spoils,* and appears with those ornaments, which extort, even from them that are most of all disaffected unto it, a confession of its most charming majesty."

The noble service to mankind, thus propounded, having been so far pursued, it is easy to imagine, that a person of but common abilities, applying himself unto it, might accomplish a very *rich collection of illustrations*, upon the glorious *Book of Truth and of Life*. It may not be amiss, but the treatise now in our hands may very agreeably do it, that the friends of learning and religion be now ADVERTISED, of a moderate performance, which by the help of Heaven, has been produced, of such a tendency.

No little part of what has been written on the great intention of *illustrating the divine oracles*, has been perused. Some hundreds of the *latest*, as well as of the *oldest* writers, that have had anything looking that way, have been consulted. Many thousands of their *finest thoughts* have been found out, extracted, and digested. The *eye* of the author's industry, has not yet *seen every precious thing;* yet it has often, in the three lustres [4] of years, which have ran since he began his undertaking, *visited the place of sapphires*, and *found the dust of gold*, which is here exposed unto the refined part of mankind, when it shall see cause to accept thereof. And there are two competent volumes of the choicest ILLUSTRATIONS (in *folio*) now lying ready for publication.[5]

The work interferes not at all, with the two very valuable volumes of the POLAN *annotations;* [6] but may ask for it, as an agreeable honor, to attend upon them.

It is hoped, that all impartial Christians, of whatever denomination or subdivision in Christianity, will esteem it, *an useful work;* for it must needs be so, if the books, from which the *best things* are fetched, and laid here together, were so.

To bestow the censure of *pride* and *vanity*, on the proposing of such a work for publication, would be therewith to reproach all attempts in such a way to serve the public. 'Tis no trespass against the rules of *modesty* (but it would look like one against the rules of *equity* to call it so) to give the public, a report, and a tender, of what has been thus prepared. It is a *lawful* and a *modest* thing, for a man to desire, that so much of a short life, as has been spent in such a preparation, should not be *spent in vain*.

The author lives in daily expectation of his death; [7] but he dies with some hope, that the glorious Head of the Church, will stir up some generous minds, to forward an undertaking so confessedly worthy to be prosecuted.

It is fit, that they should be informed, where these volumes lie waiting to be called for. They are in a *library*, to be soon found in the *American* Boston. And this is the *title* of them.

"Biblia Americana. The Sacred Scriptures of the Old and New Testament. Exhibited, in the order of time, wherein the several and successive occurrences may direct the placing and reading of them (which exhibition alone, will do the service of a valuable commentary). With,

"I. The common *translation*, with all due modesty, amended and refined in those many instances, where an army of learned and pious men in our days, have with great *reason*, proposed it.

"II. A rich collection of *antiquities* which the studious researches of inquisitive, and judicious men in the latter ages, have recovered; for a sweet reflection of *light* upon the Heavenly *Oracles:* in multitudes of passages; and particularly in those where the *idolatry*, the *agriculture*, the *architecture*, and the art of *war*, of the former ages is referred unto.

"III. The *types* of the *Bible* accommodated with their *antitypes;* and the *Blessed Book* yielding a vast mixture of holy *profit* and *pleasure*, even in those paragraphs of it, which have sometimes appeared the least fruitful with *instruction*.

"IV. The *laws* of the *Israelitish nation*, in these *pandects of Heaven*, interpreted; and the *original* and *intention* thereof rescued from the misinterpretations, that some famous writers have put upon them. With a particular history of the city *Jerusalem*, under its wondrous vicissitudes, from the days of *Melchizedeck*, down to ours; and an account of the present and wretched condition, in which it waits the *time to favor, the set time to come on.*

"V. *Golden treasures* fetched out of those most *unlikely helps*, the *Talmuds*, and other *Jewish writers;* not only to illustrate the *Oracles* once *committed unto the distinguished nation*, but also to demonstrate the truth of *Christianity*.

"VI. *Natural Philosophy* called in, to serve *Scriptural religion*. The fairest *hypotheses* of those *grand revolutions*, the *mak-*

ing, and the *drowning*, and the *burning* of the *world*, offered. The *plants*, the *minerals*, the *meteors*, the *animals*, the *diseases*, the *astronomical* affairs, and the *powers* of the *Invisible World*, mentioned in the *Book* of GOD, represented with the *best thoughts of our times* upon them.

"VII. The *chronology* of this admirable *Book*, everywhere cleared from all its difficulties; and the *clock* of time set right in its whole motion, from the beginning of it.

"VIII. The *geography* of it *surveyed;* the situation, especially of *Paradise* and of *Palestine*, laid out; an account given, how the whole earth has been peopled; and many notable and enlightening things contributed unto this work by *travellers*, of unspotted veracity.

"IX. A sort of *twenty-ninth chapter* of the Acts; or, an elaborate and entertaining history, of what has befallen the *Israelitish nation*, in every place, from the birth of the glorious RE- DEEMER, to THIS VERY DAY: and the present condition of that nation, the relics of the *ten*, as well as of the *two tribes*, and of their ancient *sects*, yet (several of them) existing also, in the several parts of the world, where they are now dispersed, at *this time*, when their speedy recovery from their sad and long dispersion is hoped for.

"X. All *appearance of contradiction*, in the pages filled from inspiration, forever taken away.

"XI. The *histories* of all ages, brought in, to show how the *prophecies* of this invaluable *Book*, have had their most punctual *accomplishment;* and strongly established *conjectures* on such as yet *remain to be accomplished*. The most unexceptionable thoughts of the ablest writers on the *Revelation*. And the true doctrine of the *Chiliad*, brought in, as a *key*, to very much of the wealth which the Church of God enjoys in this *Book* of the *Kingdom*.

"XII. Some *essays* to illustrate the *Scriptures*, from *experimental piety*, or the observations of *Christian experience*. And many of the *excellent things*, observed in and extracted from the *Holy Scriptures that make wise unto salvation*, by the *North-British expositors*, who with a penetrating and peculiar

162

ADVERTISEMENT

search after *hints for Christian practice,* have *opened* many *books* of the Bible.

"And many thousands of curious notes, found scattered and shining, in the writings both of the *ancients* and the *moderns,* laid here together in a grateful amassment.

"All done with a strict adherence to the *principles of religion,* professed in the most *reformed churches.*

"By the blessing of CHRIST on the Labors of an *American.*"

IN TWO VOLUMES.

FINIS.

NOTES

INTRODUCTION

1. Nov. 10, 1779.
2. Perry Miller, *The New England Mind: From Colony to Province* (Cambridge, Mass., 1953), pp. 402–416.
3. Cotton Mather, *Small Offers toward the Service of the Tabernacle in the Wilderness. Four Discourses accommodated unto the Designs of Practical Godliness* (Boston, 1689), pp. 108–111.
4. Here Mather seems clearly to have been following Richard Baxter's *How to Do Good to Many: or, the Publick Good is the Christian's Life. Directions and Motives to It* (London, 1682), p. 5: "But as all motion and action is first upon the nearest object, so must ours; and doing good must be in order: First we must begin at home with our own souls and lives, and then to our nearest relations, and friends, and acquaintance, and neighbors, and then to our societies, church, and kingdom, and all the world. But mark that order of execution, and the orders of estimation and intention differ. Though God set up lights so small as will serve but for one room, and though we must begin at home, we must far more esteem the desire and good of the multitude, of city and church and commonwealth; and must set no bounds to our endeavours, but what God and disability set."
5. Cotton Mather, *Early Piety, Exemplified in the Life and Death of Mr. Nathanael Mather . . .* (London, 1689), p. 39.
6. Mather, *Small Offers*, p. 37.
7. *Ibid.*, pp. 19 ff.
8. See *Theopolis Americana. An Essay on the Golden Street of the Holy City: Publishing a TESTIMONY against the CORRUPTIONS of the Market-Place. With some Good HOPES of Better Things to be yet seen in the AMERICAN World* (Boston, 1710), p. 48.
9. *Ibid.*, p. 5. The text was Revelations 21:21. The sermon was preached on Nov. 3, 1709.

10. See A. Whitney Griswold, "Three Puritans on Prosperity," *New England Quarterly*, VII (1934), 475-493.

11. *Theopolis Americana*, pp. 13-14.

12. *Ibid.*, p. 21.

13. He did not say, "Do unto others as you would have them do unto you," but rather: "*All things whatsoever* ye would, that men should do to you, do ye even so unto them." He cited Matthew 7:12. See *Theopolis Americana*, pp. 14-16.

14. *Ibid.*, pp. 18-22.

15. Baxter, *How to Do Good to Many*, p. 15.

16. A book-length autobiographical manuscript addressed to Mather's son and concentrating on the father's devices for piety. The manuscript is in the Alderman Library, University of Virginia. Many of these passages had been copied in turn from Mather's Reserved and Revised Memorials, which have since been published as *The Diary of Cotton Mather*, two volumes, ed. Worthington C. Ford, in Massachusetts Historical Society, *Collections*, 7th Ser., VII-VIII (Boston, 1911-1912).

17. This passage is quoted, with the permission of the University of Virginia, from the manuscript Paterna, pp. 304-305. I have modernized the spelling and capitalization.

THE PREFACE

1. Possibly this obscure reference is a misprint for Minos, who became guardian of the entrance to Hades, or for Mindos, an ancient Greek colony in Asia Minor.

2. Probably Robert Boyle (1627-1691), the British scientist, whom Mather admired both for his scientific and for his theological work.

3. That is, Saint Augustine of Hippo, whose *Retractations* (427) corrected errors and misinterpretations of his earlier work.

4. Sir William Ashurst, son of Henry Ashurst and formerly Lord Mayor of London (1693). Several generations of the family took a strong interest in missionary work among the American Indians, and supported the New England Company, of which Sir William was governor, 1696-1720. With his brother-in-law Sir Joseph Thompson, Sir William is praised here for his willingness to help propagate the Gospel in America.

5. Hugo Grotius (1583-1645), the great Dutch writer, jurist, and statesman.

6. That is, empirical or experimental evidence.

7. For Ezra, see the Biblical books of Ezra and Nehemiah. Democritus was a Greek philosopher in the fifth to fourth centuries before Christ. Saint Gildas was a British teacher and historian in

the sixth century A.D.; he was called "the wisest of the Bretons" by Alcuin two centuries later.

8. In Greek mythology, Briareus is a monster with a hundred arms.

9. The Biblical allusion is to I Samuel 14:4.

10. The Biblical allusion is to Acts 23 and 24. Here Mather alludes to his own recent experience (1707) with Governor Dudley, who, when Mather criticized him, circulated evidence that Mather had formerly praised him.

11. Saint Jerome, who had studied under Mather's favorite Saint Gregory of Nazianzus (Gregory Nazianzen, ca. 329–388) in Constantinople, and who wrote a highly praised translation of the Bible into Latin, engaged in many controversies; his criticism of Origen's teaching is one of the most noted of these. Origen (ca. 185–ca. 254), to whom Mather often refers, was one of the most important of early Christian theologians.

12. Aristides the Just was ostracized in 482 B.C., perhaps because of differences over military strategy, but he was later reinstated in positions of trust. *Ephori* refers to the five Spartan magistrates who controlled the kings. Agesilaus was a Spartan king, noted for his military genius, in the fourth century B.C.

13. Perhaps this term simply refers to the ridicule characteristic of people in a riotously jolly mood for the "vanities" of the famous, annual Bartholomew Fair, but there may well be a more specific allusion to the "Bartholomew Fairings"—abusively satirical pieces circulated there—or to such caricatures as Ben Jonson's Puritan Rabbi Zeal-in-the-Land Busy in *Bartholomew Fair*.

14. Janizaries were troops in the Turkish Sultan's guard. The *Oxford English Dictionary* says the word janizary comes from the Turkish "yeni-tsheri, from *yeni* new, modern + *tsheri* soldiery, militia." Mather's pun for the new order seems to be a version of this term for soldiers who were sometimes called the New Infantry.

15. Sharp, barking sounds.

16. Valerianus Magnus (1586–1661), a theologian of the Capuchin Order, author of *Contra imposturas Jesuitarum* (*Against Jesuit Impostures*), 1659.

17. This is perhaps an allusion to Robert Calef, whose charges against Increase and Cotton Mather in *More Wonders of the Invisible World* (1700) had irritated both father and son and had embarrassed them politically for many years. The allusion could also refer to Governor Dudley, as in note 10, above.

18. Vespasian, Roman Emperor, A.D. 70–79.

19. Pappus, like Euclid, was a Greek geometer; he wrote toward the middle of the fourth century A.D.

20. Mather was full of chiliastic hope in these years—hope that the millennium was at hand—and at this time his hopes centered on the year 1716.

21. That is, turned into a replica of the Biblical promised land.

22. Mather, who had been criticized for writing too much, too fast, made this incredible apology for his idleness in his diary as well. *Terentianus Carthaginensis* probably refers to Terentianus Maurus, a Latin grammarian and literary historian, probably of the second or third century A.D. (Terence the comic dramatist was born in Carthage, but he died before Varro began to write.) Marcus Terentius Varro (116–27 B.C.) is said to have written more than 70 works, more than 600 books.

CHAPTER ONE: ESSAYS TO DO GOOD

1. This is almost certainly a misprint for *whom.*

2. See Psalms 122.

3. See I Samuel 25.

4. John Stoughton, D.D. (1589?–1639), the noted Puritan preacher, made this statement on the first page of a sermon called "The Happiness of Peace," preached before King James I and later published in *Choice Sermons, Preached Upon Selected Occasions* (London, 1650). Mather's quotation is faithful but inexact, omitting allusions to the King and courtiers in the audience.

5. That is, a place in which people admit that they have not kept their covenant to obey the Lord. See Judges 2.

6. See Luke 16.

7. Probably Hugh Latimer (1485–1555), who preached vigorously against corruption among the English clergy during the reigns of Henry VIII and Edward VI.

8. Tertullian (ca. 155–ca. 222) has been called the first great Christian writer in Latin literature.

9. Andrew Willet (1562–1621) was an English preacher and theological writer especially known for criticisms of papal authority.

10. See the first chapter of Paul's first epistle to Timothy.

11. This allusion may possibly refer to the daring escape in which Grotius was carried out of prison in a chest. Mather's biography of his brother Nathanael, on the other hand, refers to a "poor man" whom Grotius "professed to envy" because the man spent eight hours at prayer every day. See *Early Piety*, p. [xii].

12. See Numbers 21:17.

13. See Job 8:7.

CHAPTER TWO: THE DUTY TO ONESELF

1. Probably Thomas Fuller (1608–1661), English preacher and writer noted for his epigrammatic wit.
2. That is, no man repents "of his wickedness." See Jeremiah 8:6.
3. In II Samuel 16, Shimei curses King David; David refuses to punish him, insisting that he be allowed to curse, "for the Lord hath bidden him."
4. Venom was sometimes used to make antidotes, or treacle. Mather preached and published a sermon called *A Treacle Fetched out of a Viper* (Boston, 1707).

CHAPTER THREE: RELATIVE TO HOME AND NEIGHBORHOOD

1. Disney was a wealthy, religious man whose book, *Some Remarkable Passages in the Holy Life and Death of Gervase Disney, Esq.* (London, 1692), was published posthumously by his brother so that readers might "see how he was wont to exercise himself, while many of his rank are for hawks and hounds, for cards and dice."
2. Roman orator, whose panegyric to Theodosius I was written in A.D. 389.
3. This passage, which extends to p. 52, appears also in Mather's Paterna.
4. Once Mather records in his diary a remarkable coincidence. Having forgotten to name one of his three children during a private prayer in his study, he reprimanded himself for such an oversight. Just then a servant ran in to tell him the child had died an hour earlier. See Mather, *Diary*, I, 186.
5. Johann Christoph Wagenseil (1633–1705) was a German Christian Hebraist who made a specialty of publishing Jewish works that were critical of Christianity.
6. Mather had condemned the slave trade in earlier works, as he does here in the next paragraph; but twice he accepted a slave as a gift, and he once gave a slave to his father. See, for example, Cotton Mather, *Theopolis Americana*, pp. 21–22; and *The Negro Christianized* (Boston, 1706), especially pp. 23–27. Mather's own slave was a gift from Sir William Phips, Governor of the Province of Massachusetts; Mather allowed the slave to go to sea and then, on his return, liberated him. See Mather, *Diary*, I, 22, 203, 579.
7. Cf. *A Good Master Well Served* (Boston, 1696), in which Mather had expounded on the mutual duties of master and servant.

8. This seems to contradict Mather's earlier insistence that good works follow, rather then precede, justification. The idea of becoming entitled to the reward of the heavenly inheritance seems to deny that grace is a free gift. This problem, however, is implicit in all Puritan preaching that invites the unregenerate to repent or strive for repentance. If challenged with the apparent inconsistency, Mather would undoubtedly have denied that the "reward" could be a consequence of anything but faith, which must precede the kind of obedience he mentions here. Thus "show[ing] them very particularly, how" may simply mean telling them of the need to repent and teaching them some methods of seeking the grace that may or may not be given to them.

9. See Genesis 39.

10. Both these Biblical "maids" bore children fathered by Jacob after his wife, having conceived no children, sent Bilhah and Zilpah to his bed. Genesis 30, 35, 37.

11. See James 1:27.

12. Roman Emperor, 79–81.

13. See Luke 6:34, 35.

14. See Matthew 5:44.

15. A Greek church father and Christian apologist (ca. 105–ca. 165), born a pagan.

16. See Luke 6:35.

17. See Jeremiah 31:16.

18. Mather copied these two sets of rules from his own actual proposals for societies in Boston, for which he had drawn up the rules. See Mather, *Diary*, II, 24, 27, 419.

19. That is, let their names be obliterated from the roll!

20. Here, just after he has rather inconsistently suggested that religious ethics in the community has nothing to do with political questions, Mather comes closest to Benjamin Franklin's kind of emphasis: diminish controversy about theology, and concentrate on practical piety. Franklin's proposed Society of the Free and Easy extended this idea drastically, to include all men of virtue.

CHAPTER FOUR: MINISTERS

1. Philip Melancthon (1497–1560), German theologian and reformer, was closely associated with Martin Luther during the first years of the Reformation and was the chief architect of the Augsburg Confession. He insisted that good works are the necessary consequence of faith.

2. Here Mather describes his own practice from the earliest days of his adult life. From the beginning his Revised Memorials, now

his published diary, are often organized according to periodic days of fasting, prayer, and meditation.

3. See John 17:17.

4. Mather himself had at least resolved to make this true of his own social conduct. His diary and Paterna record the effort, with explicit suggestions for certain classes of people.

5. Pietro Martire Vermigli (1500–1562), a native of Florence who became Professor of Theology at Strasbourg, was strongly influenced by certain writings of Martin Bucer (1491–1551), the German Protestant reformer, who was dismissed along with Peter Martyr and others when the armies of the Emperor Charles V occupied Strasbourg.

6. Jean Charlier de Gerson (1363–1429), a French theologian, concentrated on religious education of youth at Lyons during the last years of his life.

7. Now Mather quotes again his own Paterna, begun for his first son, Increase, but then addressed to his surviving son Samuel. It had not yet been completed in 1710, and it certainly had not yet been "left" to his son.

8. This, too, is copied from Mather's own Reserved Memorials.

9. The *Pastoral* referred to was written by Saint Gregory I, in the last decade of the sixth century, on the bishop's pastoral duties. *Pastor Evangelicus* was first published by Edward Bowles (1613–1662), an English Presbyterian minister prominent in the Parliamentary service, in 1649.

10. In the 1640's, Nicholaus Vedelius also wrote on controversial questions of Church and State power, and such Puritans as John Norton of Boston defended him against Roman Catholic critics.

11. A young man named Eutychus slept during a sermon of Paul's; then he fell three stories, apparently to his death, but he was miraculously restored. See Acts 20.

12. See Revelations 2:2.

13. Probably Saint Ignatius I, second bishop of Antioch (ca. 70–ca. 107).

14. Thomas Cranmer (1489–1556), Archbishop of Canterbury under Henry VIII and Edward VI.

15. Gaon is a Hebrew word, meaning excellency, applied to the head of a talmudic academy. The "Geonins" were especially important in medieval Jewish tradition for their authoritative decisions on questions about the Law.

16. Mather himself had studied medicine. Aegidius Atheniensis, or Saint Giles, died early in the eighth century. He was thought to be an Athenian who had left his home for France in order to avoid being praised for having cured a cripple. He is the patron of cripples

and beggars. Constantinus Afer, an eleventh-century medical teacher, was also a Benedictine monk. Sigismund Albicus (1347–1427) was a professor of Medicine and royal physician at Prague for 20 years before he became archbishop. I have not been able to identify Bochelt.

17. George Herbert, (1593–1633), the poet and preacher, wrote *A Priest to the Temple; or the Country Parson*, which was published posthumously in 1652.

18. Raphael is the angel of healing, one of the seven archangels.

19. The evangelist Luke was a physician who accompanied Paul on several of his missionary journeys. He is the patron of doctors.

CHAPTER FIVE: SCHOOLMASTERS

1. That is, from ministers to teachers.

2. German Protestant biographer (1551–1622), author of *Vitae Germanorum philosophorum* (1615–1620).

3. In many Massachusetts churches, applicants for membership were required to present a public account of their conversion, usually to the elders of the congregation. See Mather's account of Indian churches in the Appendix.

4. Probably Dr. John Reynolds of Wolverhampton, England (died 1684), a friend of Richard Baxter; or else his eldest son and namesake (1667–1727).

5. This is quoted from Mather's Revised Memorials.

6. Sebastian Castalion (1515–1563), French Protestant theologian, published a Latin translation of the Bible (1551). Joannes Posselius edited Greek versions of the Gospels and Epistles (1572), and other Greek texts.

7. See James Duport, Dean of Peterborough, θρηνοθρίαμβος, *sive Liber Job Graeco carmine redditus* (Cambridge, Eng., 1637).

8. Marcus Fabius Quintilianus was a writer and professor of rhetoric in the first century A.D.

9. That is, Ajax bearing a scourge. According to some versions of the legend, the Greek hero Ajax went mad and attacked and murdered Greek sheep, mistaking them for his enemies. The title is that of a Latin translation of Sophocles' tragedy.

10. Presumably Pliny the Elder (A.D. 23–79), Roman naturalist.

11. I have not been able to identify this allusion.

12. Orbilius Pupillus was the teacher of the Roman poet Horace; through Horace's writing the name of Orbilius came to symbolize flogging and other cruelty in school.

13. That is, appeals to force (by beating with a stick).

14. That is, Well done!

CHAPTER SIX: CHURCHES

1. See Matthew 25:5.
2. Perry Miller has explained the importance in late-seventeenth-century Boston of these periodic catalogues of sin and of the ministers' "jeremiads," in *The New England Mind: From Colony to Province*. Cotton Mather wanted to continue the practice and to extend it after it had begun to decline.

CHAPTER SEVEN: MAGISTRATES

1. Saint Athanasius (ca. 295–373), Alexandrian bishop.
2. East Roman Emperor from 602 to 610, who was elevated from the lowly post of centurion to commander of the army of the Danube and who later became Emperor in Constantinople. He was soon deposed and executed.
3. See Revelations 6.
4. Gratian (359–383) was Roman Emperor from 367 until his death.
5. The language and proposals in this paragraph resemble Jonathan Swift's *A Project for the Advancement of Religion and the Reformation of Manners*, published in London, 1709. See, for example, *Bickerstaff Papers and Pamphlets on the Church*, ed. Herbert Davis (Oxford, 1957), p. 50.
6. See, for example, Jeremiah 50:29 and Psalms 7:8 and 18:20.
7. That is, religious faith and political wisdom, or the lawgiver and the practical teacher.
8. Greek poet of the sixth century B.C.
9. See the Epistle of Paul to the Romans 2:3.
10. Saint Basil the Great (ca. 330–379) became bishop of Caesarea in 370.

CHAPTER EIGHT: PHYSICIANS

1. Abraham Zacutus Lusitanus, great-great-grandson of a famous astrologer and physician of the same name, was forced to leave Lisbon at the age of 50 (1625). He joined the Jewish community in Amsterdam, where he published many books on medicine.
2. Professor of Greek at Louvain, Castellanus published this book at Antwerp in 1617.
3. The first edition of *Religio Medici* to be approved by Sir Thomas Browne, the author, was published in 1643.
4. Often referred to, sometimes as giants, in the Old Testament.

5. The greek god of Medicine.

6. That is, surgery.

7. Thomas Sydenham (1624–1689), English Puritan physician and author of two books considered important in the history of medicine.

8. A part of the "Hipprocratic Collection," by which a physician vows to honor the teachers of his art, to work for the benefit of his patients, and to keep silent about the knowledge of affairs of which he learns in the privacy of his patients' homes.

9. Sir Richard Blackmore (died 1729) was a physician who published much prose and verse, including several epics. He had attacked the wits of his day for irreligion, and he was in turn ridiculed by Pope, Dryden, and others.

10. Nehemiah Grew (1641–1712), an English physiologist, published much on comparative anatomy in animals and plants. Then in 1701 he published *Cosmologia Sacra, or a Discourse on the Universe, as it is the Creature and Kingdom of God.*

11. A Greek philosopher (371/370–288/287 B.C.), who headed the Peripatetic school in Athens after Aristotle retired. Mather's reference probably alludes to Theophrastian envy in the contemporaneous sense of mildly satirical criticism.

12. The reference is to Thomas Erastus (1542–1583), a Swiss professor of medicine at the University of Heidelberg, who published a number of theses against the doctrine of excommunication (and was himself excommunicated for a time) but whose name was then attached to a doctrine he opposed: that the interests of religion are subordinate to those of the state.

13. Probably Theodore Zwinger the Elder, but perhaps his son, of the same name. Both wrote extensively on medical subjects in the late sixteenth century. Conrad von Gesner (1515–1565) was an extremely versatile Swiss physician and naturalist. He achieved especial fame as a botanist and for his "universal" bibliography. He also published a theological encyclopedia.

14. Ancient name for Tabriz, a rich city in Azerbaijan; also, a small island off the coast of Illyria.

15. Probably Paulus Freherus, whose work was published in two volumes in Noriberg, 1688.

16. Possibly Athanasius Kirker, or Kircher (1602–1680), a German Jesuit scholar who published many works on science (including a volume on medicine), Egyptian hieroglyphics, and other subjects.

17. In John 5:2, Bethesda (or Bethsaida, or Bethzana) is a pool in Jerusalem to which the angel of the Lord occasionally descends to perform miraculous cures. Mather titled his own unpublished medical book The Angel of Bethesda.

18. Georgi Baglivi (1668–1707), author of *De praxi medica* (1696), was an Italian professor of Medicine who had a great influence on the development of therapy according to clinical experience.

19. Probably Friedrich Hoffman (1660–1742), a German friend of Robert Boyle and pioneer in emphasizing the nervous system as a source of disease. Editions of his works appeared in several languages, so that Mather's French title should not seem too strange.

20. Perhaps "Mithridates" is Mithradates VI Eupator, who lived in the first century B.C., and whose varied intellectual talents are celebrated in legend. Publius Aelius Hadrianus (76–138) was Roman Emperor from 117 until his death. Constantinus Pogonatus, or Constans II (630–668) was the Byzantine Emperor from 641 until his assassination.

21. Aulus Cornelius Celsus, who lived in the first century A.D., has been called the greatest Latin medical writer.

22. That is, ca. 130–ca. 200. Galen was a famous Greek physician who visited the great medical school at Alexandria. There, Mather suggests, magical cures were attempted.

23. Perhaps Mather's reason for saying "Hence" is that the Greek word "pharmaca" meant *poison* as well as *drug*, and that it might thus be associated with magic.

24. Eusebius of Caesaria (ca. 260–ca. 340) was an important historian of the early Christian Church, who wrote also on other religions.

25. See I Kings 21.

26. See II Kings 9:15.

27. See II Chronicles 16:12.

28. By George Bate, M.D. (London, 1688).

CHAPTER NINE: RICH MEN

1. See Mark 12:42.

2. See Genesis 28:22.

3. See Genesis 14:20.

4. See Hebrews 5:6.

5. Xenophon (430–after 355 B.C.) was a Greek historian; Herodotus, the great Greek historian of the fifth century B.C.; Pausanius, a Greek traveler and geographer of the second century A.D.; Diodorus Siculus, a Greek historian of the first century B.C. The Doughty referred to is probably John Doughty (1598–1672), a popular and successful preacher. Sextus Pompeius Festus was a Latin grammarian of the second or third century A.D.

6. See Ecclesiastes 11:1.

7. See Proverbs 3:9, 10.

8. Thomas Gouge, *The Safest and Surest Way of Thriving* (London, 1673). Gouge worked much and systematically among the poor, and he was especially successful in giving them work to do, paying the losses himself.

9. See Malachi 3:10.

10. Mary Rich (1625–1678), Countess of Warwick, was a pious Puritan who contributed heavily to religious causes after inheriting her husband's estate.

11. Patriarch (609–616) of Alexandria, who was widely known for his charitable gifts.

12. Emperor at Constantinople, 578–582, praised for his tolerance as well as his charity.

13. See Proverbs 19:17.

14. See Isaiah 58:6.

15. See Psalms 41:2.

16. Joseph Allein, *Alarm to the Unconverted* (London, 1673).

17. That is, Mather himself. The record is estimated in his *Reserved Memorials* and again in *Paterna*.

18. Mather himself had taken advantage of such opportunities when, for example, his father-in-law, recovered from a dangerous illness, expressed his thanks to the Lord by subsidizing the publication of *Small Offers toward the Service of the Tabernacle in the Wilderness* (Boston, 1689). Note that Mather advertises his *Biblia Americana* to prospective donors at the end of *Bonifacius*. Here in the text, he seems to be hinting broadly that he would like to have financial help for publishing his other writings.

19. A portion of the Old Testament prepared by Origen in the third century—a Hebrew text and seven Greek versions of that text.

20. Robert Sanderson (1587–1663), was a remarkably effective preacher, chaplain to Charles I; later, when suffering under the Puritans, he was defended and assisted by Sir Robert Boyle.

21. The name of the library at Oxford University.

22. Probably Edward Leigh (1602–1671), Sir Charles Wolsely (1630?–1714), and Edward Polhill (1622–1694?), who wrote on general questions of piety and theology though they were not ordained ministers.

23. *A View of the Soul* (London, 1682), has been attributed to Richard Saunders.

24. Ambrosius (died ca. 250), a deacon, later bishop of Mediolanum, was the disciple and friend of Origen.

25. Henry Jeanes (1611–1662) was considered a witty, practical writer on religious questions. Mather probably knew his *The Work*

of Heaven Upon Earth (1649) and *A Mixture of Scholastical Divinity with Practical* (1656).

CHAPTER TEN: OFFICIALS AND LAWYERS

1. The commander of an enomoty (a band of sworn soldiers), in the Spartan army.

2. Sir Edward Coke (1552–1634), John Vaughan (1603–1674), Edmund Wingate (1596–1656), Michael Dalton (died 1648), and Joseph Keble (1632–1710), all wrote important works on English law, and Dalton also wrote a book on the "decay" of the Roman Church until Luther's time. Vaughan's *Reports* . . . were edited and published by his son Edward in 1677. The volumes referred to a few lines later are: Johannes Corvinius, *Enchiridion: seu Institutiones Imperiales* (Amsterdam, 1649), and Sir Arthur Duck (1580–1648), *De Usu et Authoritate Juris Civilis Romanorum* . . . (London, 1653).

3. Johann Heinrich Alsted (1588–1638) published encyclopedic works, which relied heavily on the theories of Peter Ramus.

4. Justinian I was Byzantine Emperor from 527–565, for whom Tribonian codified the law. Suidas was a Byzantine lexicographer, probably in the latter half of the tenth century.

5. Francesco Accorso, or Accursius (ca. 1182–ca. 1260), was an Italian jurist whose commentary on Roman law was considered authoritative until Bartolo da Sassoferato, or Bartolus (1314–1357), wrote a new commentary on the Justinian Code. Guillaume Budé, or Budaeus (1468–1540), was a French humanist scholar who wrote on law as well as other subjects.

6. See Job 4:21.

7. Tully is the name often used for Marcus Tullius Cicero (106–43 B.C.), the great Roman orator, writer, statesman. Mather puns on Biblical and Roman laws. The ten tables containing the Roman law were composed in 451 B.C. A year later, two more tables were added. The Baldwin referred to here is probably William Baldwin, a mid-sixteenth-century English poet whose *Treatise of Moral Philosophy* (1547) was published in many editions during the next hundred years.

8. The reference may be to Charles de Saint Denis Marguetel, Seigneur de Saint Évremond, a refugee in London from the France of Louis XIV, and author of *Comédie à la manière des Anglais, or Sir Politick Would-be* (1662). The English version of his *The Works of Petronius Arbiter* (London, 1713), p. 250, includes a poem arguing that Cerberus, the dog of Hell, was a lawyer.

9. Domitius Ulpianus (died ca. 228) was a Roman jurist who

wrote a number of commentaries, including a *Digesta* or digest of the laws.

10. The famous British judge (1609–1676), who sometimes wrote on religious matters and whose authority both Cotton and Increase Mather had cited on procedural questions during the Salem witchcraft trials.

11. Joannes Baptista de Sancto Blasio's *Tractatus . . . contradictionum juris canonici cum jure civili* was published in several editions in the sixteenth century.

12. Heinrich Cornelius Agrippa von Nettesheim (1486–1535), German physician, philosopher, and student of alchemy, who also served as an advocate, criticized many of the beliefs of the medieval Church in his *De incertitudine et vanitate scientiarum* (Antwerp, 1531).

13. Jean La Placette wrote many works on Christian ethics in Mather's lifetime, including *Traité de la Restitution* (Amsterdam, 1696).

14. Gaius Sallustus Crispus (86–ca. 34 B.C.), Roman historian.

15. By Cotton Mather, grandson of the subject. John Cotton (1584–1652) was one of the most important leaders of the first generation in the Massachusetts Bay Colony.

16. Perhaps the teacher to whom Paul wrote the Biblical epistle.

17. Written by A. Booth, *Examen Legum Angliae: or Laws of England Examined by Scripture, Antiquity, and Reason* was published in 1656.

18. William Prynne (1600–1669), was an English Puritan who wrote much on law and religion. John Selden (1584–1654) wrote on various questions of English and international law; he was one of the most important legal writers of the century.

19. Mather characteristically puns with the author's name and the Scriptural metaphor. Peter King, Lord Chancellor of England, published *An Enquiry . . . into The Primitive Church* (London, 1691) and *The History of the Apostles' Creed, with Critical Observations* (London, 1702).

20. That is, a verdict saying, "We don't know of any blemishes."

CHAPTER ELEVEN: REFORMING SOCIETIES

1. Societies for the Reformation of Manners began to thrive in England just after the Revolution of 1688, when there was little other organized welfare work except the new charity schools. Dissenters and Anglicans worked together in these societies, which seemed a new experiment. Unfortunately, they tended to work in a negative way, prosecuting in the name of righteousness and what

we now call deterrence, but they also worked positively to keep men out of trouble. Jonathan Swift reports an interesting rumor of their failure in his *A Project for the Advancement of Religion, and the Reformation of Manners:* "Religious Societies, although begun with excellent intention and by persons of true piety, are said, I know not whether truly or no, to have dwindled into factious clubs, and grown a trade to enrich little knavish informers of the meanest rank, such as common constables, and broken shop-keepers." See *Bickerstaff Papers and Pamphlets on the Church*, p. 57.

2. Written by Mather himself. See *Diary*, I, 419.

CHAPTER TWELVE: DESIDERATA

1. I believe this sentence fragment should be part of the preceding sentence, qualifying the rhetorical question or exclamation. But I have reprinted the sentence as it appears in the first edition, so that the meaning will not be distorted without warning.

2. Probably Robert Gordon (1580–1661), geographer.

3. Tyrannius Ruffinus (ca. 345–ca. 410) was a Latin theologian who translated Origen, Saint Basil, and Saint Gregory Nazianzen. Frumentius and Aedesius were brothers captured as boys by the Ethiopians and eventually elevated to high religious and scholarly office; Frumentius became the first Ethiopian bishop. The Socrates who wrote about these brothers was the fifth-century historian (born at Constantinople) of the early Christian era.

4. See John Flavel, *Husbandry Spiritualized; or, the Heavenly Use of Earthly Things* (London, 1669).

5. Mather did write The Angel of Bethesda, but it was never published in his lifetime. Large portions have been published in Otho T. Beall, Jr., and Richard H. Shryock, *Cotton Mather, First Significant Figure in American Medicine* (Baltimore, 1954).

6. Mather corresponded with Auguste Hermann Francke (1663–1727), German pietist, who founded, endowed, and supervised several schools in Halle. The *collegia pietatis* was originally a group of meetings in the house of Philipp Jakob Spener (1635–1705), founder of German pietism, teacher of Auguste Francke, and founder, with Francke, of the University of Halle. A less favorable view of one of Francke's schools at Halle is given in J. E. Hutton's *History of the Moravian Church* (London, 1909), 177–183, which condemns the school's mistreatment of young Count Zinzendorf, a pious boy, very much like the young Cotton Mather.

7. This plea might refer to any or all of three Edwardses who preached in seventeenth-century England: John Edwards (1637–1716), who wrote *A Brief Vindication of the Fundamental Articles*

of the Christian Faith . . . from Mr. Locke's Reflections upon them in his "Book of Education" (1697); Jonathan Edwards, D.D. (1629–1712), who defended the doctrine of original sin (1711); and Thomas Edwards (1599–1647), whose *Gangraena; or a Catalogue and Discovery of Many Errors, Heresies, Blasphemies, and Pernicious Practices of the Sectaries of this Time* . . . (1646) helped to solidify his position as the "young Luther" of Puritan England. The greatest Edwards, the American Jonathan, was seven years old when Mather made this plea.

CHAPTER THIRTEEN: CONCLUSION

1. Pompey the Great (106–48 B.C.), the Roman general and triumvir, was a man of considerable vanity who insisted on unprecedented public recognition after some of his great military achievements.
2. See Job 16:9.
3. See II Samuel 22:30.
4. Richard Baxter (1615–1691), one of the most influential ministers and religious writers of England during Mather's youth.
5. That is, of Cain. See Genesis 4.
6. The minister was Mather himself. The dying man had sent for him "very late at night." Samuel Mather says the name of the dying man was George Fielding. See Samuel Mather, *The Life of Cotton Mather* (Boston, 1729), p. 64.
7. That is, satirical playwrights (or others) who will ridicule your work.
8. Saint Caecilius Cyprianus (ca. 200–258), bishop of Carthage, a man of unusual charity.
9. Compare Benjamin Franklin's dialogue, published in *The Pennsylvania Gazette* in 1735, "A Man of Sense," reprinted in *The Papers of Benjamin Franklin*, ed. Leonard W. Labaree, II (New Haven, 1960), 15–19. The argument in this paragraph of Mather's is very close to Franklin's central ethical argument in *The Autobiography of Benjamin Franklin*.
10. See Matthew 7:17, Deuteronomy 29:9, and I Kings 2:3.
11. An ugly, foulmouthed character in the *Iliad*, who torments Agamemnon until Odysseus (or Ulysses) intervenes.
12. Here Mather describes himself. In Paterna he wrote a virtually identical "Testimony," but in the first person.

APPENDIX: EFFORTS TO CONVERT THE INDIANS

1. By Cotton Mather (London, 1702).

ADVERTISEMENT: *BIBLIA AMERICANA*

1. Probably Andreas Masius, editor of a seventeenth-century Polyglot Bible and of several Biblical commentaries. Joseph Mede (1586–1683) was a remarkably versatile English scholar. Sir Francis Bacon (1561–1626) was the great herald of the "new philosophy" of modern science.

2. Joannes Magirus, M.D., wrote a number of medical books in the early seventeenth century. Bartholomeus Eustachius' sixteenth-century works on anatomy were published in many editions.

3. Mather called H. Witsius, professor in the University of Leyden (died 1708), "one of the greatest men that the last age produced." Witsius wrote commentaries on the Bible and on the Apostles' Creed (1700). Mather confided to him his own plan for *Biblia Americana,* and said later that Witsius had encouraged him to proceed. See Cotton Mather to John Woodward, Nov. 17, 1712, in the Royal Society, London.

4. That is, 15 years.

5. They still lie waiting to be published, at the Massachusetts Historical Society.

6. Probably Mather refers here to Matthew Poole's unfinished *English Annotations on the Holy Bible* (1679). He had alluded to them in his biography of Nathanael Mather.

7. Mather was 47 years old when *Bonifacius* was published. He lived another 18 years.